Our
Twelve Days
Before Christmas

Our
Twelve Days
Before Christmas

Christopher White

ECW PRESS

Published by ECW PRESS
2120 Queen Street East, Suite 200, Toronto, Ontario, Canada M4E 1E2

NATIONAL LIBRARY OF CANADA CATALOGUING IN PUBLICATION
White, Christopher, 1956–
Our twelve days before Christmas / Christopher White.

ISBN 1-55022-614-2

1. White, Christopher, 1956 – Anecdotes. 2. Christmas – Anecdotes.
3. Authors, Canadian (English) – 20th century – Anecdotes. 1. Title.

PS8595.H417O97 2003   C818´.5403   C2003-902202-1
PR9199.3.W55O97 2003

Developing editor: Jennifer Hale
Cover and Text Design: Tania Craan
Cover illustration: ©Werran/Ochsner/Photonica
Interior illustrations: Wesley Bates / Three in a Box Inc.
Production and typesetting: Mary Bowness
Printing: Transcontinental

High Tech Santa
Words by Angela Darter Stogsdill
Music by Cristi Cary Miller
Copyright © 1997 by HAL LEONARD CORPORATION
International Copyright Secured   All Rights Reserved

This book is set in Bickham Script and Columbus.

The publication of *Our Twelve Days Before Christmas* has been generously
supported by the Canada Council, the Ontario Arts Council, and the
Government of Canada through the Book Publishing Industry
Development Program. **Canada**

DISTRIBUTION
CANADA: Jaguar Book Group, 100 Armstrong Avenue, Georgetown, ON, L7G 5S4

PRINTED AND BOUND IN CANADA

ECW PRESS
ecwpress.com

To the women who fill my life with joy and love all the year round:

my wife, Wendy, daughters, Sarah and Elizabeth;

my sister Alison,

and in memory of my mom, Jane.

CONTENTS

On the Sixth Day

before Christmas, my true loves hid from me
six Christmas items that I kind of, sort of, hope
they might put under the enormous pine tree. *105*

On the Fifth Day

before Christmas, the call went out from me for five
Thespian goats (and please keep them away from
the enormous pine tree). *123*

On the Fourth Day

before Christmas, we practised at the church with
four- and five-year-old shepherds, who fought
under the enormous pine tree. *143*

On the Third Day

before Christmas, Mother Nature gave to me three feet of
snow that blanketed the enormous pine tree. *161*

On the Second Day

before Christmas, the choir sounded to me like two
calling birds nesting in the enormous pine tree. *181*

On the Last Day

before Christmas, I paused and gave great thanks for the
manger under the enormous pine tree. *197*

ACKNOWLEDGEMENTS

A book such as this does not spring to life in isolation but comes from the love and support of those who surround the writer. That was certainly the case for me. My first thank-you goes to my wife, Wendy, for her boundless love, patience, and support. Her help as my first editor was invaluable. Next in line are my daughters, Sarah and Elizabeth, who put up with Christmas carols being played from the frost of December to the heat of July as I wrote each day and who came to understand the roller-coaster nature of this kind of work.

I feel truly blessed for the support and friendship of Don Bastian, first my editor and now my agent. He has believed in this book from its inception and faithfully guided and shaped it as it came into final form. I am deeply grateful to Jack David, Jen Hale, and Joy Gugeler and everyone at ECW Press for their enthusiasm and support. Stevie Cameron was extremely generous with her time and wisdom. My colleagues and congregation at Westminster United Church never wavered in their support — and, of course, they supplied much of the material I wrote about! Thanks to my friends at CBC Radio, Shelagh Rogers, Shelley Ambrose, Tom Allen, and the late, wonderful Peter Gzowski, all of whom encouraged me to share my stories. And thanks to the folks at *Whitby This Week*, who ran my column for all those years and were understanding about my constant reinterpretation of the word *deadline*.

Finally, special thanks to my sister, Alison, who makes our Christmas every year by coming home each December; my father, Patrick, who showed me how to write and modelled the effort and sheer determination that goes into each page; and my mother, Jane, who loved this season above all and is missed whenever our family gathers around a table.

BEFORE THE COUNTDOWN

It starts in late August. It is a steamy, hot day, so hot that you leave footprints in the asphalt as you make your way across the parking lot and into the Canadian Tire hardware store. You prowl the aisles looking for sun block with an SPF of about five hundred and bug repellent that could gag a grizzly for that last camping trip of the summer. As you gaze around, you are stunned by the transformation. Everything that calls out summer has been removed with indecent haste, and fall and winter have materialized. You make your way to the seasonal section, and there before your unbelieving eyes you see them. Boxes of tinsel, garlands, and glass ornaments centred on a two-foot-high singing Christmas tree, which actually dances in its stand to the tune of "Santa Claus Is Coming to Town." You exit screaming, sobbing, "Not yet, please, please, not yet," and drive off hoping that sunstroke caused a hallucination.

By Labour Day, all is forgotten, and before you know it Thanksgiving has come and gone, and you are staring Halloween right in the face. But by the time you have composted your pumpkin and come down after a two-week-long sugar high from sneaking your kids' candy, it can no longer be put off. The Christmas season is upon you.

You think about all that has to be done: the shopping, the decorating, the entertaining, the concerts. But there is so much time left; there's no hurry. You hear people talking about how they finished their shopping in June, or found that perfect gift two months ago, how all their wrapping is completed and their Christmas cards and parcels ready to go. A slight tremor of concern flickers through you, but you dismiss it and them with a disdainful shrug. "They don't understand the Christmas spirit at all," you say, comforting yourself. "They miss the whole meaning of the season by doing everything so early." When the time is right, at just the right moment, you will spring into action, and then everyone will see what a real Christmas is about.

But you don't spring, you hardly move, and now it is December 13. You have just twelve days before Christmas. The time of reckoning has come for me, my wife, Wendy, and our daughters, Sarah and Elizabeth. Complicating matters is the fact that I am the pastor of a church, Westminster United Church: the craziness of Christmas at home is doubled or maybe trebled by the craziness of the season at church.

On the Twelfth Day before Christmas,

my true love gave to me

an eight-foot, enormous pine tree.

Twelve days! I have twelve days left to create the Christmas to end all Christmases, a Christmas that even Charles Dickens would salute. There is, of course, only one place to begin: the tree.

The selection of the Christmas tree is the critical single event that defines the whole season. Pick just the right one, and joy abounds. Your children ooh and aah. Your spouse looks upon you with pride. Your neighbours gather to pay you homage. But get it wrong, and woe betide you. Your children will peer sadly at its drooping branches, its gaping holes, and your half-hearted remarks about a Charlie Brown Christmas tree will pass unnoticed. Your spousal unit will give you that steely eyed look signifying that if you were a hockey player you would be on the trading block for the rights to a spouse to be named later.

The pressure is on, and you must respond to the challenge.

The first issue is where to get the tree. Some will suggest that there is nothing more bracing, no activity more in keeping with the spirit of the season, than getting everyone into the car and going to a cut-your-own tree farm. Yes, you, the latter-day urban lumberjack, can stride through the fields, pick out the tree, and fell it with a few quick draws of the saw. But beware: there are hidden complications when you cruise through a tree farm.

My wife and I discovered that for ourselves, just after we were married. We wanted to start our own tradition, one that would distinguish our household right from the beginning.

Feeling that close newlywed emotional bond, we drove out to where I was sure there was a cut-your-own tree farm. Finding it hidden away among the concession roads northeast of Toronto proved to be the first hurdle of our adventure. We got lost. To be truthful, I got us lost. But I did have some assistance. Mildly critical words were exchanged in the car, a map was sent flying in the direction of my head, and when we finally arrived it wasn't just the weather that was a tad chilly.

But we cheered up and walked and walked and walked some more, examining each tree judiciously until we found the Scotch pine that seemed perfect. Feeling like a true Canadian lumberjack, I started to saw away at the trunk . . . and then the blade got stuck a third of the way through. Wrenching the saw free, I approached the tree from the other side. Again the blade got stuck. My image as a manly, capable male, a hewer of wood and drawer of water, was taking a beating. I hacked away at the evergreen with growing desperation, until finally I yelled "Timber!" and proudly watched our five-foot tree sail gracefully to earth. We hauled it out of the bush and tied it on top of our hatchback. With that sense of pride that comes from surviving the primeval forces of nature, we took it home.

Back at the house, as we prepared to put the tree up, I noticed in the centre of the trunk, right in the middle, what appeared to be a bird's nest. "How wonderful," I thought. "Just the place to put our ceramic doves."

The next morning it became clear that the birds had flown and another of God's creatures had taken up habitation. I was in the kitchen making toast when out of the corner of my eye a small brown blur appeared and then disappeared as if by magic. I shook my head. I must have imagined it. Later that night I heard a scratching sound — now, apparently, my ears were playing tricks on me. By the next day, we had irrefutable proof that we were no longer the sole occupants of our home. We had a roomie, a small furry creature with a tail, that no doubt believed there really was a Santa Claus, as he was now residing in a home that provided food and shelter.

What to do with our guest? He was a mouse, but he was an official Christmas mouse. He had to be removed but in a way in keeping with the spirit of the season. I opened the front door. Armed with a broom, I prowled the kitchen, where I knew he was hiding. Opening the cupboard and brandishing bristles, I swept him toward the door.

Chasing a mouse around the kitchen with a broom does not enhance one's Christmas mood. I leaped; he leaped. He dashed toward the living room; I cut him off at the pass. He ran down the hall; I sprinted in hot pursuit. He looked to the stairs but saw that Wendy was descending them and came back in my direction. I bellowed and brandished my broom. Like a crazed curler, I cried, "Sweep, sweep!" He had no other option: he dashed out the door and into the suburban wilderness.

That marked the last time we cut our own tree. But it did signal the beginning of an annual event, the battle of the Christmas tree.

Like all rituals, this one has evolved over time, and new dimensions have been added with the arrival of our two daughters. Having eschewed "cut your own," Wendy, the girls, and I head out every December to the nearest Boy Scout tree lot.

Once we arrive, every tree must be meticulously examined. How does it look? Is it tall enough? Is the trunk straight? What will it look like when the branches drop? Is there a bare spot? What about the one buried at the bottom of the pile that hasn't been unwrapped yet? That could be the one.

It takes less time for most people to buy a car than for us to purchase a tree. But just when frostbite is becoming a serious concern, we find our prize, an eight-foot Scotch pine that barely fits on top of the car, let alone in the house. We no longer want a tree to just grace a home. No, we like it to totally dominate the environment.

And so I bring the tree in and lean it up against the wall in the hall, there to await us while we quickly put our hitherto innocent and happy children to bed. The girls are under the impression that Christmas is a time of endless joy and smiles. They are too young to be disillusioned. There are some festive sights that are simply unsuitable for the little ones — no, not seeing their parents kissing under the mistletoe, but watching them put up a Christmas tree.

But I was optimistic. After a decade of using buckets of sand and cast-iron instruments of torture, I had purchased a simple, well-engineered, and well-balanced Christmas-tree stand. I was confident that I would finally be able to put up the tree in a painless, marriage-enhancing, and stress-free manner.

After countless years of my snapping, "Hold it straight; it's shifting," and Wendy replying, "You want to hold it straight? Do it yourself," and exchanges of other terms of endearment, I dreamt of effortlessly slipping the tree into the stand, twisting a few screws, and then, in a hazy balm of Christmas joy, sitting in front of the fire for eggnog and a cuddle.

It started off so well. I hauled in the tree, put it in the stand, turned it around a couple of times so that its bare spots would be against the wall, and smiled in a loving, encouraging sort of way at Wendy. She then held the tree while I attached the screws.

Now an eight-foot Scotch pine has a fairly thick trunk, and my *It's a Wonderful Life* mood soon began to evaporate as I inhaled dust from the carpet, was prickled by pine branches, and worked my fingers raw turning the screws. But finally all was done, and I stood back and admired my handiwork.

"Let go, Wendy," I said. "It's perfect."

I looked with satisfaction at our accomplishment, a huge conifer rooted to our living room floor. But as I watched it standing tall and straight, a tiny, hardly noticeable tremor ran through the tree. At first I thought it was my imagination: perhaps an errant breeze was rustling through the branches. But the tremor did not stop there; it grew, vibrating as though the aftershock of an earthquake had shaken the room.

Wendy, oblivious to it all, was standing with her back to the tree. I could see where this was headed. At that precise moment, the tree shuddered, gave a loud creak, and, with the majesty of an ocean liner sinking into the depths, began its descent to the floor, right on top of Wendy.

In one motion, I leapt and grabbed Wendy, and together we descended onto the couch as eight feet of evergreen came crashing down with an impressive whoosh and thump. My heroic gesture was misinter-preted.

"Christopher," she admonished with an arched eyebrow. "The girls aren't in bed yet!"

I rolled off her and onto the floor, picked up the tree, and looked at my beloved regretfully.

"Sweetie, I think you neglected to hold it perfectly straight."

"Darling," she responded, "if you remember, I did mention that the tree was on an angle."

With infinite patience, I replied, "But love, if you had held it straight, it wouldn't have been on an angle."

By now her hazel eyes were starting to flash, so I picked up the tree. She held it again; I redid the screws; she let go. Whoosh. Thump. We tried again. Whoosh. Thump.

"There's no need to swear like that," Wendy said. "You'll wake the girls."

I got out the hammer, nails, and binder twine; we fiddled with the tree, hammered some nails into the baseboards, and then tied it up. This time I held the tree while Wendy fastened the screws. She stood up. I held my breath and let go. It stood alone, quivering for a moment, but it stayed standing. The time for eggnog and a cuddle was now long past, but civil relations were restored, and we headed for bed.

I remember one morning in particular during this

phase of our tradition. The girls admired our handi-work before breakfast.

"Is big, Daddy," said three-year-old Elizabeth.

"It looks great, Dad," added six-year-old Sarah.

Later, as we shared the morning paper, I looked up at Wendy and asked, "Where's Elizabeth?"

Our minds sharing a single thought, we leapt from the table and ran into the living room. Elizabeth was behind the tree, stepping over one of the support lines.

"No-o-o!" I shouted.

Startled, she hit the cord. Whoosh. Thump.

I actually entertained plans from then on to get a tree that comes in a box. However, I have been told that even that kind of tree has its hazards. It's like putting together a three-dimensional jigsaw puzzle for which everyone is an expert on which part goes where. And if you get the branches mixed up, you get to start all over again. Apparently, there was no easy way out of this.

Human beings have been dragging members of the evergreen family into their homes since the dawn of time. The whole thing started as a way of marking the new year. Flowering shrubs would be brought in, and it was hoped that they would blossom as a sign of new life in the dark of winter. Since this didn't always work out, people moved on to evergreens, which were always, well, you know, green, even in the darkest, coldest months of winter.

The Germans really got things going about 1605, when the first official Christmas tree made its appearance. Decorated with apples, paper roses, and candies, it became an instant tradition. When Queen Victoria married Prince Albert, he brought the concept from his native Germany. Standing only two feet high and placed on a tabletop, the Christmas tree swept the country and the British Empire. Everyone had to have one, and everyone did.

But excuse me? Two feet tall? That's not a tree, that's a shrub, a branch, an overgrown pine cone. A tree, a real, honest-to-goodness Christmas tree, should require a forklift truck and a crane to get it into your house or through your balcony door. For when it comes to trees, size (ahem) does matter.

A few years ago we got the biggest spruce tree in our family history. We forgot our living room was not the same size as the Boy Scout Christmas tree lot. I saw the tree. It called to me, "Take me home, take me home." What could we do? Leave it all alone in a cold, cold parking lot? So, as the girls jumped up and down, Wendy and I convened an emergency meeting regarding our differences on the correct species of tree. We negotiated the following agreement: we would annually alternate tree species. One year would be spruce, the next year would be Scotch pine.

Peace broke out, and, with the help of Brenda from the Scouts, the massive tree was manoeuvred onto the roof of the station wagon. With four-way flashers going, we drove regally through the streets of Whitby and took it home.

The next morning we removed it from the garage and began the challenging job of relocation. As we hauled this monster into the house, two things happened. First, the stipple on the ceiling started to fall as the top of the tree made grooves through it. Second, my chiropractor called, reminding me of my missed appointment. I assured her she was going to get a lot of my business after I got the tree up. Then I took the saw to remove part of the top of the tree so we could get it upright.

With the CN Tower of trees before us, peace reigned. We strained our backs getting it in the stand; it leaned, it fell. I hammered extra shims into the stand with a screwdriver (I'd lost the hammer) to support the tree and tied it with enough ropes to keep a rampaging bull at bay. But through it all, everything was calm. No language was spoken that couldn't appear in a family publication. We were joined together in a sacred task. We knew that this tree was bigger than both of us, that without total cooperation we would never get it upright. After many, many tries, it rose off the carpet like a Saturn rocket heading into orbit. It swayed slightly, as though a gust of wind from its home forest had hit it. But it stood, a one-tree forest that looked like it was preparing to engulf the whole house. A couple of hours later, with an extra string of lights, two boxes of tinsel, and every decoration we owned, it was ready. I knew in that moment that we had chosen absolutely the right tree, because a real, live, honest Christmas miracle occurred in our house: for this one year, there was no battle when we installed the tree in our home.

The next day Wendy's piano students walked in, and their jaws dropped. Neighbours wondered how we'd actually got it in the house. How big was it? Nine feet tall with the angel on top and six feet across at the bottom. But don't trust me; we brought in scientific experts to confirm the actual size. I consulted my friend Mark from down the street. Mark is a physicist by trade. You can trust his calculations.

First, the circumference. As we all know, pi times d equals circumference. Pi is 3.14; pi times 6 equals a circumference of 18.8 feet. The radius is pi times r squared, r is 3, r squared equals 9, 9 times 3.14 equals 28.3 surface square feet at the base.

In other words, it was big — very big. I had absolutely no idea, once the branches had dropped, how on Earth we were going to get this behemoth out of the house without major renovations. But that was a problem for the new year.

Now we come to this Christmas, with twelve days to go.

Earlier this month, I kept driving by the parking lot where the Scouts have sold their trees since time immemorial. But instead of the fence and the trailer that signified the imminent arrival of the trees, all I saw was bare, windswept asphalt. The only signs of Christmas were discarded store flyers that swirled about like confetti.

"Don't worry," said Wendy, "they always arrive late in the season. They'll be there."

But I did worry. I run to a precise and tight time line when it comes to the purchase of the tree. Like the Boy Scouts, my motto is "Be prepared."

So when there were no trees, I called the Scouts. Their reply heralded the end of civilization as we know it. A grand part of the very fabric of our society was no more. Its loss signalled the collapse of one of our great family Christmas traditions. What was this calamity? The Boy Scouts of Whitby had stopped selling Christmas trees. What, I ask you, is this world coming to when we are all faced with a Scoutless Christmas?

Early in our marriage, after our one rodent-enriched, cut-your-own experience, Wendy and I went to one of two favourite Scout lots in Toronto, at Christ Church Anglican at Yonge and St. Clair, or at St. James Bond United at Avenue Road and Eglinton. When we lived in Calgary, we found Scouts selling trees, and when we moved to Whitby there was the lot on Brock Street, right by Jerry's Drug Store.

On the first Friday the trees went on sale in Whitby, we would be there. The tree would be purchased, taken home, and left propped up in the front hall. We would then take the girls to Cullen Gardens garden centre to see the lights and the show and have a quick visit with Santa. The perfect pre-Christmas evening.

But no more. When I talked to a Scouting acquaintance, she told me the sad truth. The Scouts in Whitby were losing money selling the trees. The supply was uncertain, disease was a problem, they just couldn't do it any longer.

Catastrophe! What were we to do? Where were we to go? Surely somewhere in Durham Region there must have been some Scouts willing to sell us a tree? I phoned Hugh, the dean of Scouts. He called me back with the sad news that the closest Scout tree lot was in Toronto, in Leaside. Leaside? Can you imagine barrelling home on the eight lanes of the 401 with a nine-foot tree on top of an Escort wagon?

Where were we supposed to go? What were we to do? Fortunately, the Kiwanis Club came to our rescue. It sells trees in front of Kingsview United in not-far-off Oshawa. And so, on a freezing Friday night with the snow blowing, we drove over. Within a few minutes, we found it, our tree, the perfect tree, tall at the top and broad at the base, right at the back of the pile. We paid for it, felt satisfied that the money was going to support a worthy cause, and took it home.

I descended to the basement, rooted through the Christmas boxes, and extracted the stand. The plastic rim near the screws had worn away and would no longer support the tree. So off to the store I went in search of a new stand. Upon my arrival, I was presented with a bewildering selection of choices. There was your standard plastic, water-filled, wide-base type and some very traditional-looking stands. But what really caught my eye was a flashy model made of space-age polymer plastic with a rotating bucket insert and a foot lock so you didn't even have to crawl under the tree and get a face full of needles. It looked too perfect, too easy. I was suspicious. There had to be a catch. So I selected a red metal stand made in New Brunswick that had a large seven-by-seven-inch bucket with four very large support screws and took it home.

Retrieving the tree from the garage, we attached the stand, we lifted up the tree, and before we knew it that spruce stood as strong and tall as if it were still in the forest. In other words, no spousal battle, no squabbling about holding it straight, and no attaching cables to keep it upright. No annual Christmas tree fight. I'm not sure this is a healthy development.

I mean, if husbands and wives can't release the pre-holiday stress on a safe, neutral subject like a Christmas tree, where will that stress go?

We survive the loss of the annual argument. But I still miss those Scouts. And, Wendy, that wreath, you're not hanging it straight, here, let me help . . .

Overnight the tree branches will drop, and it will be time to decorate. This is a Herculean task that makes the selection of the tree mere child's play by comparison.

On the Eleventh Day before Christmas,

my daughters gave to me

eleven paper angels to decorate

the enormous pine tree.

The time has come for the decorating frenzy. It's not enough that we bedeck our trees with ornaments and other baubles. Our homes have to resemble Santa's workshop on steroids: lights bright enough to be seen from Mars, bows, wreaths, not to mention indoor crèches, miniature Dickensian villages, and replicas of Father Christmas beaming from our mantel tops.

This important piece in the puzzle of Christmas begins when I step into the open air and begin putting the Christmas lights on the house. This is a great winter event, one that finds me standing on a ladder in the freezing cold on the first weekend of every December. Each year I ask myself the same question: "Why didn't I have the sense to just leave them up all year round?" The effort of taking them down is hardly worth it. As soon as I actually get to the point of removing them, sometime in early June, it's just a few months before I have to whack them back up again. So why not simply leave them there? I could change the colours to fit the seasons: green for spring, yellow for summer, orange for fall. It would save time and inconvenience, not to mention bruises, scrapes, and contusions from ladders and the various architectural features of my house.

But still, year after year, up I go. Putting up the outdoor lights is still one of those jobs reserved primarily for the male of the species. This time of the year you can find us wobbling on ladders, clambering on rooftops, and hanging over eaves, all to drape the lights in that absolutely perfect spot.

It is competitive out there in my festive neighbourhood. With other homes displaying ribbon lights, icicle lights, in white or multiple colours, the pressure to measure up is intense. Do I use lights to outline the front of the house and the peak of the roof? Or do I include every tree, bush, and plant larger than a dandelion on the property? Then there are statuaries. What about adding a reindeer or a glowing Santa? And maybe the outline of a sleigh with Rudolph at the front? Where is the Martha Stewart of Christmas lights when you need her?

Once you start the process of assembling your exhibit, it can be dangerous. If the fever hits, you keep adding string after string until the house is so brightly lit that the people next door have to keep their blinds closed at night so they can sleep.

If enough members of the same neighbourhood share the fever, beware: your street will become a regular stop on the local Christmas light tour. In this seasonal ritual, the whole family piles into the car and rides around the community finding the best outdoor light displays. Woe to you if you have made the hot-spot list, for the consequences can be dire. The evening traffic will clog your street, and every neighbour's driveway will turn into a parking lot as people get out to ooh and aah over the results of your creativity.

I know of one house in Calgary that had so many visitors the police turned the streets into a series of one-way thoroughfares until after New Year's. The man's electricity bill was so outrageous he had to sell photographs of his illuminated house to help defray the costs.

But in my region, the most famous drive is to the east, to a place called Old Scugog Road, in Bowmanville. This stretch of houses is either your dream or nightmare of the perfect holiday neighbourhood. Each house is a Christmas card of lights and decorations. There are around fifty houses so bright that passing aircraft can use the area to mark their approach to the Oshawa airport. Traffic is intense, with cars and tour buses slowly driving up one side and down the other. No house is left unlit. In fact, I think there's a municipal bylaw that forces you to relocate if you don't put up an impressive display.

To date, I have avoided going to such extremes. I am a simple traditionalist, one who has resisted the siren call of icicles or ribbon lights and multi-coloured spots that flash on and off. I possess only four strands of brightly coloured bulbs. One goes along the front eaves. Three go in the trees and bushes in front of the house. That's been my limit. But I confess to eyeing my twenty-foot pine tree on the corner of our lot with increasing interest, and I keep wondering about the potential of the blue spruce beside it. I could add a set of blinking lights to outline the fence and do something creative with the wisteria on the side. Highlight the apple trees in the backyard, put a backlit partridge near the top of my plum tree (close enough to a pear), a star above the garage, and three illuminated wise men on the garage door. Put the aforementioned Santa up by the chimney, add a few reindeer, and we're set. You see? The madness can affect anyone.

The actual assembly of the lights is a test of patience and stamina. Fruitlessly, I search my memory for the place I stowed them last year. I check the basement, examine the garage, pull apart the front cupboard in the hall. Perhaps they are camouflaged by the kangaroo-sized dust bunnies down by the freezer or buried under some insulation up in the attic? It's a game of hide-and-seek. The hunt is punctuated by my plaintive wail: "Wendy, do you know where the lights are?" Finally, I find them, stuffed on the back shelf in the garage, behind the old aquarium used in the failed goldfish-as-the-perfect-pet experiment.

The lights lie there hissing at me, tangled together like a ball of snakes. The first job is to get that mess unsnarled. I call the girls out. Strand by strand, we straighten out the twisted ball of cords and bulbs. That takes a good thirty minutes as I attempt to lay them out in straight lines on the front yard. Working as a well-integrated team, we get ourselves totally ensnared by the lights, crushing at least a dozen bulbs, until the strands are draped over the snow-covered lawn.

Next I bring the ladder out, and with my daughters hanging onto it for dear life — my dear life — I make my climb. The real joy of this enterprise is that the ground is uneven, so the ladder teeters on an angle. If the earth is not yet frozen, you can compensate by jamming the side of the ladder into the ground. If it is frozen, you need a pickaxe to make a dent in it. When you add in my lifelong dislike of heights and the rash I get from the two spruce trees that flank the house, it's an afternoon of total delight.

Halfway up the ladder, I call to Santa's helpers, "Sarah, Liz, stop talking and hold that ladder straight." Clutching the lights in one hand, holding tight to the ladder with the other, I ascend to the heights. There is a definite wobble in the structure bearing my weight. "Girls, hold it steady," I bellow down.

"I am," says Sarah.

"So am I," challenges her sister.

An argument now breaks out as to who is actually holding the ladder properly. I ignore it all, climb onto the roof, and place the lights around the eaves and over the peak, being extremely careful to keep my eyes on the job.

In the distance, a telephone rings. I immediately sense danger. "Wait," I cry. "Let your mother answer it." Too late; both of my helpers are off at warp speed into the house. Left wobbling by their haste to get to the phone first, the ladder tips over. I am trapped, all alone on top of my roof.

The wind whistles as I gaze out over the streetscape. I see other men engaged in the same task; their ladders are standing at attention. I hear a "caw, caw," as a crow lands on my chimney. The bird looks at me speculatively, calculating how long I can survive on my own up here. If there were vultures in Whitby, they would be circling by now. I have a teenager on the phone and no provisions, no food, no water. I could be here for days.

The sky is darkening, snowflakes start to fall, lights are coming on, dinners are being served. In frustration, I start pounding on the roof. "Dad!" I hear two voices in unison. "Oh, no, he's still out there." Back they come and pick up the ladder, and I descend, growling. I grab more lights, then go back up the ladder, from tree to bush, until all of them are installed.

Once it is done, I call Wendy to come outside. Then I plug the lights in. We gaze admiringly as our house lights up. It is only then that I realize the top bulbs on both the spruce trees and the roof have gone out. As I clamber up to replace them, I make a mental note for the eleventh year in a row: plug the lights in and check them *before* they go on the house.

Frozen solid but filled with seasonal joie de vivre, I head inside, where Wendy has been busy setting out the interior decorations.

Of all the Christmas ornaments and accessories that we have in our house, my favourites are the two Advent trees that sit on the sideboard in the dining room. Advent is the four-week season before Christmas, historically used as a time of preparation for the big event. Our trees are made of wood, cut and painted in the shape of a Christmas tree. Each stands about a foot high, including the yellow star on the top. They have twenty-five small finishing nails that are hammered halfway into the front, with a small number painted over them. Each one holds one LifeSaver candy. Every day during Advent our daughters eat a LifeSaver until they get to the star on the top of the tree on Christmas Day. We got the trees at the craft fair in Springbank, Alberta, when I was the minister of that community's United Church. We had just discovered that our elder daughter, Sarah, was extremely allergic to dairy products, nuts, eggs, and peanuts. The traditional Advent calendar with its chocolate windows wouldn't do. We needed a substitute. So we heard about the Christmas craft fair and headed down to the high school gym late one November.

The Springbank fair had that Alberta feel that made it utterly unique in our experience. When we arrived, the building was packed with shoppers and artists. Everything you could possibly imagine was on display: oil and watercolour paintings from local artists, homemade afghans and quilts, brass sculptures of cowboys on bucking broncos, decorations of every description, seasonal foods, candies, and preserves, and even hand-tooled cowboy boots. In the midst of the crush, we discovered a booth that specialized in tole painting. There in front of us sat the Advent tree. We couldn't believe our good fortune and snapped it up. Three years later our second daughter, Elizabeth, was born, so back we went to the fair in search of another tree. If you have two daughters, from time to time family harmony requires not simply parity but also perfect symmetry.

We found the booth, we found the artist, but, alas, the market for Advent trees was not robust, and she had made no more. Before us rose the image of Christmas after Christmas with only one Advent tree between two girls. It was not a pretty sight. Future conflicts over whose turn it was to get the LifeSaver seemed inevitable. We had only one option. We begged, we pleaded, we made our case for peace and goodwill to all, or for our family anyway, if she would provide us with one last Advent tree. She sympathized, but she had neither tree to give us nor the inclination to create another.

Just as we were pushing our stroller away, she called out. "Wait. I think I have one more, I just remembered. It's in the basement, a little marked up, but would that be all right?"

Would it? We were thrilled. Later that day she called us at home, and we drove over and picked up the tree. One scratch at its base but otherwise perfect. My babies are now fourteen and eleven, and we have had a decade of joyful Advents. No matter how old they get, they expect those trees to be put out and filled with LifeSavers on December 1.

Of course, we have many more decorations in the house. A fabric picture of the angels singing to the shepherds, a Rudolph made of wooden spoons, our two crèches, one ceramic and one fabric, perfect for children to play with. The fabric one was given to us by our wonderful and sadly missed friend Kathy Kerr from Springbank. It was sewn by one of Wendy's piano students' moms and is vibrant with colour. The ceramic crèche was given to Wendy by her parents. Now that the house is bedecked with these and wreaths made over time by the girls, we can turn our attention to the main event: decoration of the tree itself.

Two angels will sit on the top of our tree. One,

with wings consisting of a lace doily cut in half, is a paper figure with a smiling face, hands folded together, hair coloured yellow, its body a variety of crayon colours inexpertly applied. At the bottom it says "Sarah '91." She glued and coloured that angel with all her love and energy when she was three years old. The second paper angel is a seasonal crayon green with swirly cardboard wings and a beatific smile. It was a Sunday school creation by Elizabeth.

We have more elaborate angels professionally crafted and artistically created. But we have none that is as beautiful or as meaningful as these battered paper angels that grace our tree. They smile down at us, reminding us of a stable, a baby, a moment when angels sang to frightened shepherds and hope was born in a troubled world. I love these angels and all the decorations that go onto our tree. Each of them tells a story, a story about our family, a place, a time, a moment.

Down in the basement behind the furnace sit three large boxes with a variety of smaller boxes on top of them. For fifty weeks a year, they stay silent, unnoticed, gathering an impressive layer of dust, the sounds of spring, summer, and fall passing them by. Then, on this the eleventh day before Christmas, they are opened to great fanfare. We hold up each decoration, piece by precious piece. They are examined, and their stories are told. With much negotiation, they find that perfect place on the tree, that place where they were meant to be, and there they sit, giving joy and pleasure to all who see them.

There is, of course, a proper order to follow in decorating the tree. The lights are the first to go on. You might think this is a walk in the park compared with my rooftop adventure, but you would be wrong.

I go back to the garage, get the stepladder, set it up parallel to the tree, and then reach over and attempt to attach the first light onto the top branch. The key is not to overreach, or gravity, that implacable force, will take hold of you, and you will discover whether an eight-foot pine tree can both hold your weight and remain standing upright. Chances are the answer is no. You and the floor will be covered with a tree and the gallon of water in the stand. This will necessitate resetting the whole tree, if not purchasing a new one. So, with great care, I grasp the top branch, jab my fingers, drawing small to medium quantities of blood, and force that first light on, just below where the angels sit. Once that is done, I strategically pass the lights to my spouse, who winds them halfway across and around the tree. She passes them back over to me, and I finish the loop. Around and around I go, draping the tree in lights.

It is critical not, I repeat not, to fasten them at this point. This is because a fierce debate is about to take place on the correct placement of the lights. While the annual putting-up-the-tree argument is limited to spouses only, the light placement is a family affair. Everyone on this round table has an opinion as to where the lights should go, helpfully pointing out the gaps that must be filled and the correct way to drape the lights. Since I am the only member of the family who is over five foot three and a half, I'm the one who gets to arrange the lights according to three different sets of simultaneous instructions. "Lift them over there; you're missing a branch." "That doesn't look quite right." "There are too many bulbs the same colour close to each other."

Once consensus has been reached, approximately two hours after we began the task, the lights can be attached. The wonderful thing about the attaching process is that because of my height I get to rearrange the lights the way *I* think they should go. When that's complete, Wendy scoots up the ladder and rearranges them once more, just before the girls try to head on up and correct both of their parents' shortcomings. Once this is finally done, the lights are turned on, and joy abounds.

In the ancient days of my childhood, I watched my father struggle with his lights, get them on the tree, then scream primeval oaths when they failed to go on once plugged in. This is because, in historic times, when one bulb burned out the whole circuit was broken, and you had to test each socket with a fresh bulb to catch the miscreant. These days the worst that can happen is that a single bulb goes out, necessitating an easy replacement. Well, most times. Occasionally, one of the bulbs will decide that, after residing in that socket for three or four years, it has no intention of being moved. It is so stubborn that it breaks off at the stem. I then have the pleasure of attempting to extract the bulb without breaking the whole socket. I rush in with pliers and a kitchen knife to convince the remains to shift.

What is absolutely key in this whole procedure is not to get overexcited and, in my zeal to remove the end of the bulb, forget to unplug the lights. Or, even worse, have a spouse or child plug them back in at the precise instant that the needle-nose pliers make contact with the socket. There is nothing like forty volts zipping through your body to bring you closer to the spirit of Christmas past — your past. In addition, the sight of me chasing my child all over the house in order to discuss her recent actions does not enhance the Yuletide ambience.

Once the smoke clears and the vibrations throughout my body slow to the occasional twitch, it is time to apply the garland. There are two opinions on this. One holds that a garland is superfluous, that tinsel will suffice. The other holds that tinsel is nothing but a cheap and tawdry display, long on flash, short on substance, while a garland is elegant, flowing beautifully throughout the branches. Then again, tinsel shimmers, it shines, it escapes from the tree and can be discovered in every nook and cranny in your house throughout the year. It becomes a constant reminder of the festive season. What could be better than that?

Many newly married couples have found their first Christmas fraught with tension over such questions. There is shock or horror when one spouse realizes that the newly acquired mate does not share every tradition. It grows worse as they face the truth that each family has distinct ideas about holiday celebrations. Tinsel and garlands can be but the thin edge of the wedge, leading to other thorny issues such as the correct time to open gifts (Christmas Eve or morning) and whose family gets what part of the day with whom. Heated words may be exchanged; suggestions that your partner has no idea what makes a true Christmas may be made.

When we were newlyweds, Wendy and I had an issue over the type of decorations to put on the tree. We purchased a box of glass balls, and I brought them to our apartment triumphantly. Much to my surprise, once the package was opened, a significant discussion ensued in our household. Wendy came from a home where there were satin-covered balls, which have the advantage of being unbreakable. I, however, came from a house where my mother's stated goal was to have a tree that sparkled like a diamond. Hence the glass balls. Wendy's argument that they could break if they were dropped or if the tree ever fell down was dismissed with disdain. The tree fall over? How would that be possible? Was she actually questioning my manly expertise in putting up the Christmas tree?

When we came home from work the next day to discover our newly erected tree prone on the parquet floor — with my glass ornaments broken and rolling around the living room — I had to concede that she had a point.

As with all issues of this nature in a domestic relationship, the answer is never "either/or" but "both, and." Thus, in our home, garlands *and* tinsel grace the tree, there are glass *and* satin balls, and we see *both* families on Christmas Day but alternate the dinners. This last arrangement evolved after years of having an early dinner with one family and a later dinner with the other —a practice that added ten pounds to each of us over the holidays.

And so, with these issues safely resolved, the garland is draped, and now the main event is upon you: the full tree decoration.

You can tell the age of a household by the appearance of the tree. If the fir primarily sports paper chains and cardboard bells, chances are that there are small children or grandchildren in the house. A secondary clue is the spread of decorations.

If they are all evenly placed throughout the tree, then the children are older. If, however, the bottom two feet are stuffed with balls, angels, and hand-painted ornaments, then this is a house full of preschoolers.

The first boxes of decorations opened in our home belong to the girls. Wendy has bought them a decoration each year, so when they leave our house and set up on their own their Christmas will be ready. (A note to any future husbands of my daughters. Congratulations! No dowry but some boxes of Christmas baubles! What else could any man ask for?)

Once the girls' ornaments are brought out and laid on the couch, we open the other boxes, and the stories begin. There sits the very first box of decorations Wendy and I purchased together. The famous set of glass balls painted like poinsettia plants. This box would best be described as the faithful remnant, with many casualties over the decades since their purchase. The rest of the tree is covered in an eclectic combination of decorations from a wide variety of places. Craft fairs are one of our favourite places to buy them.

All craft fairs are irresistible; each has a unique flavour. The aforementioned Springbank fair had its special features, and our present church, Westminster United, has its. My church has a baking table where marvellous butter tarts are on offer, but you have to get there early, for they disappear in minutes. Your only other option is to have friends in high places. More than one package of my favourite confection has mysteriously made its way to the pulpit on a Sunday morning. The home knitting is second to none, and sweaters, mitts, and hats are popular items with the folks who crowd the tables. Lunch is available in a café area set up near the kitchen: homemade soups and sandwiches, all brought to your table.

This event gives Wendy and me a chance to compare notes on what has to be accomplished in the days ahead. Wendy always buys some decorations here, one for each of the girls and one each for our stockings. So many, in fact, that we will soon be forced to add a second tree just to hold them all!

But each of our decorations has special meaning. From our years in Alberta, we have a beautiful hand-quilted ball made by my friend Lil Purcell. Lil's heart was as big as the Alberta sky, and she made that for us on our first Christmas after Sarah was born. From the Springbank United Church bazaar, a couple of white paper stars and a horse. My love of birds is reflected in the silver peacock my mom gave us, the ceramic doves we found early in our marriage, and the six brightly coloured birds that came from El Salvador. In their glorious reds, greens, and blues, they bring a vibrant life to our tree. The gold ball my mom gave us is matched by other decorations that came from her, such as the dish, the cow, and the spoon from the nursery rhyme. Our uninvited Christmas visitor is commemorated with decorations of mice hanging on candy canes, mice in ballet costumes, and a mouse in a stocking.

Then there's the homemade Popsicle-stick reindeer, quilted candy canes, tinfoil bells, and sparkling pine cones dipped by the girls. Picture balls with photos of the girls at various stages of their lives, musical instruments — a saxophone, a couple of trumpets — reflecting Wendy's work as a music teacher. Paper chains in red and green. Angels big and small, made of paper, cloth, coloured silver, gold. Wooden sleds, a cork horse, various candy canes, brass stars, and snowflakes, which are always the hardest ornaments to find when the tree is finally taken down. Santa on a sleigh, Santa bearing gifts, an old Victorian-style Father Christmas, miniature Christmas baskets filled with gifts. Ballerinas from *The Nutcracker* or the girls' dance studio craft fair, Victorian paper fans, wooden Christmas trees, two decorations for Sarah and Elizabeth from my sister's trip to Bali, made from shells and beads. Of course, there are the girls' first Christmas ornaments, marking their births. Then there are the cardboard stars and bells that finish the tree off to perfection.

As we decorate the tree, some of our favourite music goes on: James Galway's flute, Fred Penner's guitar and voice, a little Raffi for nostalgia's sake, and, for me, the Cambridge Choir's version of Lessons and Carols. When the last decoration is put on, Wendy carefully analyzes the whole effect and pronounces judgement. It is the best tree our family has ever had. She gives us handfuls of tinsel, which we enthusiastically throw on the tree. We turn on the lights and stand back in complete wonder. It glistens, the lights glowing and reflecting the tinsel and garland, each branch covered in a myriad of decorations. It's simply beautiful and worth every splinter, every argument, every face full of pine needles. We sit and watch, silent but for the carols playing in the background.

By now it's totally dark, and dinner is waiting. We light the second Advent candle and pause to catch our breath. Tomorrow will be busy enough.

On the Tenth Day before Christmas,

my true love gave to me

ten shopping lists for kith and kin

with enormous pine trees.

You can no longer put it off. Plans must be made, strategies implemented. The season for Christmas shopping is upon us, a time of year when fear fills the hearts of the bravest of men. A time when all of us can be found clutching parcels, with that half-stunned, half-hopeful look that says, "I hope they like it. Nothing says love like kitchen appliances." You think that I exaggerate? You believe, here at the beginning of the twenty-first century, that things have changed, that we live in a different world now? Ha.

I well remember the days of my first solo Christmas mall expeditions. The only people I had to shop for were my parents, my sister, Alison, and my girlfriend. I lived in Toronto at the time. I would make the list, a list that would fit on a single scrap of paper, then walk over to the subway and take it downtown to the Eaton Centre. I always timed my trip precisely to fall on the Saturday before Christmas. Since it was my one shopping trip of the year, I had my own rituals. I really enjoyed the crowds, thousands of people moving through the stores, each trying to find a gift that would bring a smile to a loved one.

If you were a Canadian of the postwar generation, Eaton's was not just a store; it was also part of your identity. The Americans had Macy's and Gimbel's. We had Eaton's and Simpson's. If you shopped at one, you rarely shopped at the other. They both had huge (by the measure of the times) stores downtown. Eaton's would signal the beginning of the official Christmas shopping season with its wonderful parade, which would snake through the city on a Saturday in late November. Simpson's would counter with animated windows. These imaginative creations were filled with seasonal scenes: Santa's workshop, reindeer in training, Santa delivering presents, all with electronically moving puppets. I remembered loving these scenes as a child, working my way through the crowds to the front of the window, utterly enchanted by what lay before my eyes.

I would start my shopping in Eaton's, looking for a toy for Alison or later a record or some other critical item of teenage paraphernalia. Of course, there were also the stocking stuffers. Shopping for stocking stuffers is an art all of its own. In our family, to this very day, my sister and I have an annual battle to see who can purchase the most fiendishly difficult puzzle to put in each other's stocking. I have shopped far and wide for them. They are the one item I look for all year long. This past Christmas I discovered a triangular Rubik's cube. Each side has to be the same colour before it is completed. Alison never had a chance. She hurled it in my general direction after a few hours of fruitless attempts and after a few of what I considered to be helpful suggestions. A few weeks after Christmas, when we were having a postproduction Christmas play cast party, a couple of teenage boys found the puzzle (strange how it never made it into Alison's suitcase) and solved it in under an hour. I sent Alison a picture of me holding the finished puzzle in my hand, with my tongue sticking out at her. Brothers will be brothers. By the way, no need to tell her that I didn't actually do the puzzle myself.

Once I had my sister's gift, I would seek out pipe tobacco, cigars, or comb honey for my dad or maybe a book. For Mom, her favourite Taboo perfume, bubble bath, a Christmas decoration, and anything to do with cardinals, her favourite bird. If I was stuck for a gift for Dad, then a trip up the street to A&A's to buy him a classical record might follow.

If Eaton's and Simpson's defined the department store divide in the Toronto of the time, A&A's and Sam's marked the competition in the record world. This was the time when vinyl was king. Cassettes were just over the horizon, CDs were in the realm of science fiction, and the only challenge to actual records lay in the new eight-track tapes, which were about the same size as a VCR tape (if you can still remember *them*). Sam's had the edge on rock music and a fantastic collection of 45s, those two-sided records that would hold a hit single on one side and a throwaway tune on the other.

Both stores had huge storefronts downtown on Yonge Street with flashing neon signs that drew customers from all over the city. But if you were an aficionado of "serious" music, you would head to A&A's. The second floor, after the noise and bustle of the first floor, where teenagers lounged around the record bins arguing over the various merits of each artist, was like another world. It was a hushed and serious place. Customers spoke in muted voices and looked at a teenage male with surprise and suspicion. Where downstairs you could wander for hours without being bothered by a staff person, upstairs you had about two minutes before you were approached. You thought you were going to have to show your birth certificate to prove you were old enough to be in that part of the store.

After I had authenticated my bona fides, I was accompanied around the floor as we attempted to find a recording that would satisfy my father's Wagner craze. Having considered numerous alternatives, I secured a record intended to have the rest of the family cursing me for months, something like *The Best of Fafner*, the dragon that is featured in Wagner's Ring Cycle.

Then it was time to move on to that trickiest of

purchases. The girlfriend gift. This was a potential minefield. It had to be something thoughtful, tasteful, and affectionate, something personal. But not so personal that, when she opened the gift, her outraged father would throw you out of the house and promise to set the dog on you if you were ever so foolish to attempt to reestablish contact.

But the rocky shoal upon which many a romance has crashed is the issue of parity. How much was she going to spend? What was she going to get you? For instance, if she purchased a gold ID bracelet with your name engraved on it (the only acceptable male jewellery of the time), and in response you gave her the latest offerings from Deep Purple, you were done like the Christmas turkey.

The role of boyfriend is a nebulous one; you have no real standing. To the family of your girlfriend, you are but a temporary fixture, quite possibly soon to be replaced by a newer, shinier model. Since all boyfriends are essentially there on a consignment basis, they are reluctant to invest too much in a gift, since they may never see it or the girlfriend again. But woe betide you if you make a serious misjudgement, as happened to me one year.

I had grazed the shoals the previous Christmas and put a scrape on my hull, but there had been no need for the lifeboats. I had been thoughtful but "economical" in my purchase. My girlfriend, on the other hand, had been extremely generous, and more than one gift was put before me. I was shocked and filled with a sense of impending doom. There was no place to hide. I needed another gift and fast. I could stall, pretend I'd left it in the car, and speed off to the closest mall. Or look surprised and say that her other present was at home, then flee the premises. Or, even better, suggest that it would be delivered after Christmas since, due to the wild popularity of said item, it was on back order. All these ideas flashed before me in an instant and were rejected. I squared my shoulders and told her how grateful I was for her generosity and how much she meant to me. Stay of execution. I was not dumped for my indiscretion.

The next year I did what all men should do in a similar circumstance and headed to the jewellery counter. I purchased a gold oval locket and necklace, then picked up a small bottle of perfume.

I would be all set. With my purchases complete, I would haul my parcels to the food court, buy some lunch, and then, with the milk of human kindness splashing around me, head back to the subway. On the way home, I'd give up my seat automatically for seniors (known at the time as people who were old), and everyone returning home from shopping, though exhausted, would have the same air of tired satisfaction.

But that was then. This is now. A very different time,

with much longer lists. There are children, in-laws, outlaws, nieces, nephews, your wife, and sundry family members. Our current annual task has taken on a whole new complexity. I suggest that it be planned as you would a major expedition, something like climbing Mount Everest for the weekend. Lists need to be made, equipment secured, and a mutually agreed-on plan of attack drawn up. We in the 'burbs never take the subway because, alas, we don't have one. And the buses appear as regularly as UFO sightings. Thus, the vital first element in today's mall expedition is securing the perfect parking spot.

Malls, as we know, contain acres and acres of parking spots, none of which is available at Christmas time. The only spots are so far away that it's a two-day overland trek to get to the front door. If you have your children with you, you are finished before you even enter the mall. That parking lot walk alone wears them out. The instant you enter the store, the words "Mommy and Daddy, I'm tired, can we go home now?" are spoken with increasing volume and urgency. To prevent this, you must master the parking lot cruise. Some people make the mistake of driving around waiting for somebody to vacate a spot. This is a rookie error. The experienced among us know that you have to troll for spots starting right at the mall entrance. Slowly, you drive by the door looking for customers burdened with packages heading for their cars. You follow one to his or her spot, hit the flashers, and claim the territory.

Research has shown that people vacate their spots much more slowly when there is a car waiting to take over their real estate. This is even truer in this season of the year. Drivers cling to their corners of asphalt like zebra mussels to rocks in Lake Ontario. They can't bear to surrender their prized property. In fact, sometimes the worst happens: they drop their packages in their cars and go back for more, leaving you high and dry.

Once you have finally secured a spot, you enter the mall and are immediately hit with oxygen deprivation. This gives you a feeling of tiredness, combined with an overwhelming desire for a large cinnamon bun and a coffee. As at the top of Everest, mall air is thinner. Don't panic: you will acclimatize. Walk slowly, breathe deeply, and review your lists. As with all expeditions, your equipment is critical, so dump your coats in a locker or the Salvation Army coat check. Shoppers wearing winter gear never make it. You find them panting in the aisles or outside stores — victims of heat prostration.

You are now ready to enter what I call "the flow." This is a highly dangerous manoeuvre. The flow of people heading through a mall is like the tide, remorseless and unstoppable. Why, just last Saturday, I saw a family of four attempting to walk in the opposite direction of the crowds. Before they knew it, they were caught. The last I saw of them, they were being swept toward The Bay, vainly clutching for each other. Not a pretty sight. You have to gauge the moment and then jump right in and move with the multitude.

It is important as you begin shopping to avoid the temptation to divide the lists. This is deadly. When your spousal unit suggests meeting you at a certain time by Santa's castle, refuse outright. Otherwise, you will never see each other again. Spouses will find themselves caught in a three-hour lineup for something that wasn't even on the list, and you will simply have to abandon them to their fate. Stay together; there is safety in numbers.

At some point, food will be required to replenish your resources. The food court cruise is another unique art form. This is the one time you have my permission to divide your party into two groups. The first has the food orders in hand and goes to the kiosks to purchase them. At this time of year, it is absolutely essential to share a single food theme — Mexican, pizza, Chinese, or falafels — anything, as long as you have to stand only in a single lineup. The other part of your team searches out the landscape for a table. This is similar to the parking spot hunt but more intense. Speed and accuracy are critical. Once you spot a table of people whose trays are filled with empty plates, you hover like a predator on the African plains. As soon as the current inhabitants shift their knees, signalling their intention to stand up, you swoop in. You must claim the space while the previous party is still leaving. Timing is absolutely imperative; clambering across their laps as they stand up, while regrettable and somewhat embarrassing, is but a small price to pay. For you have only a nanosecond, and, if you wait for them to actually lift their trays from the table, another family will swarm in, and all will be lost.

Twelve hours after you arrived, the last challenge awaits: the return to the parking lot. You exit the mall only to find that the trail of crumbs you left to guide you to the car has been eaten by hungry shoppers who couldn't get seats at the food court. This is when Sherpa guides truly would come in handy. But you don't need one, because you are an expert. You know that the only way to survive is to make your automobile recognizable from afar by attaching a marker to the antenna. A large ribbon or a small Canadian flag (my friend Irene makes them) waving from the top of your car allows you to safely and happily identify and get to your vehicle. While other families wander the parking lot, calling to each other ("It's over here — no, there it is!"), you drive away to your happy home. It is only when you pull into your driveway that you realize your coats are still at the mall.

There are, as we all know, two types of Christmas shopping. The first is for all the adult members of your extended family. The second, the one that parents dread more than anything else, is shopping for the children. Toy shopping adds a whole new layer of tension to the holiday retail experience. I know, for I, too, have lined up at the crack of dawn to get that one toy that must be under the tree. For instance, just a few short years ago, I was sent out to do battle because of a toy sale of outstanding value at one of the local department stores. Wendy had to stay home with Elizabeth, who was a preschooler at the time, so I was dispatched with a list and a store flyer in my hand.

"Remember," Wendy said, "you have to be there right at 9:30 a.m., when the store opens, or it will be too late."

I didn't believe her; I figured that by noon should be fine, but just to humour her and for the sake of marital harmony I went on time.

As I arrived at the store, I discovered that I was not alone. About forty people were milling about, waiting for the doors to open. They, too, clutched flyers and lists, and we looked at one another suspiciously, recognizing and measuring the mettle of the competition. Shamelessly, I manoeuvred myself close to the front. Women with children in strollers eyed me with open animosity. I tried to look unconcerned.

It was simply a case of survival of the fittest.

Finally, the doors opened, and like a herd of stampeding buffalo the price-crazed consumers surged forward. I grabbed a cart and led the pack to the toy department.

During the dash to the back, a small child was bodychecked into the menswear department. Without breaking stride, his mother picked him up and kept moving. I admired her. Now that was fortitude: others would have abandoned him to the wolves. We rounded the final corner and saw cowering before us some store personnel, brandishing their flyers in a vain attempt to keep us at bay. But we smelled success, and within seconds these poor souls were absorbed by a mob screaming, "Where are the Aladdin dolls?"

I swept down the aisles, my eyes cold, my heart stern. I recognized that this was a case of take-no-prisoners shopping. By now all the doors had opened, and it was total chaos. The air rocked with the noise of battle, the clash of shopping carts, the cries of "It's mine; I saw it first!" and the sounds of the wounded, wailing, "Do you give rain checks?" Occasionally, I spotted a fellow male looking grim as he filled his cart. But for most of the other men, it was all too much. They floundered about at the back, looking like beached trout.

Methodically, I worked through my list. With

everything accounted for, I attempted to head out. Within thirty minutes, it was all over. The shelves had been decimated, inventory swallowed whole. It was as if a plague of locusts had swarmed through the store, leaving nothing but battered boxes and last year's toys. I was truly sorry. Nothing was left for Christmas for anyone else. We got it all.

At the checkout counter, the survivors traded stories like veterans of a natural disaster. One woman looked at me and said, "I would never send my husband; he's too passive. Why, he'd let people take things right out of his cart." There was much head-nodding. Apparently, I had struck another blow for gender equality.

As I returned to the office, I realized something: I had no idea what the toys I had just bought looked like. In my haste, I had grabbed whatever I could take. I had no knowledge of size, shape, or colour. At the thought of having to make an exchange, I broke out into a cold sweat. Even warriors have their limits.

So, girls, now you know why, on Christmas of '93, you each got two Aladdin dolls and no Princess Jasmines.

On the Ninth Day before Christmas,

my daughters gave to me

nine concerts to remember,

so I collapsed under the enormous pine tree.

"Christmas at times is like a freight train. We're all on it, and there's no way to get off." So said a minister this past Sunday. As I was that minister, I can't help but agree with that insightful and wise analogy. School concerts, choir concerts, piano recitals, ballet demonstrations, skating competitions — they all seem to gang up at the end of the year. You need three Palm Pilots and a couple of Day-Timers just to keep up.

This year's train ride began last Sunday night at our annual Carols and Readings service. The church was candlelit; the music was seasonal and moving. It is one of my favourite services of the year. But instead of being calm and relaxed, I was tense and stress filled. Why? Because at the same time the Whitby Youth Choir was having its Christmas concert at another church across town. My daughter Elizabeth was making her concert debut. Since her show started thirty minutes after our service began, and her choir was slated to perform near the end of the evening, I estimated that if our service ran sixty minutes on the nose I would have time to leap in my car and make it just as they took to the stage.

"You will be there, won't you, Daddy?" asked my youngest, whose eyes can melt a father's heart.

"I'll do my best," I told her.

As the service began, I promised myself that I would not look at my watch. It's bad enough to see someone watching the time during a sermon, but it's even worse if the preacher is checking to see how long it's been!

Fortunately, I played only a minor role in this worship service and so was able to sit in a pew beside my friend Jim the Ticket Wizard. Jim is a magical person able to secure tickets to all sporting events, especially the games of our hometown NHL team, the Toronto Maple Leafs. Since these tickets are as rare as seals in the Sahara, he is the man to know. If you have any question about any hockey player, Jim will have the answer, as he will invariably know or be distantly related to the player's father. I must add my congratulations to Jim, who is now a future father-in-law, as his eldest daughter just got engaged. Yes, Jim, Leafs season tickets are the perfect wedding gift, every bride's dream. (Well, if not the bride's, then certainly the groom's.)

In any event, Jim was wearing his watch, and every time he stood up when we sang a Christmas carol it ticked away at me like Big Ben. But I resisted temptation and averted my eyes . . . mostly.

The service drew to a close, and as I rose to pronounce the benediction I slipped a quick look at the time. We were nine minutes over, 540 precious seconds beyond my scheduled moment for departure. I had six minutes until my youngest was due on stage, six minutes until she was looking out across the bright lights for her father's face. I didn't panic — I was somewhat dignified, my exit a trifle faster paced than usual as I made my way to the back of the church. Then I burst into the lobby, grabbed my coat, and ran to my car, strategically parked right outside.

About a week before, Wendy and I had seen the latest James Bond film. I learned two things from that movie. First, I am too old for James Bond. I discovered this because my elder daughter is starting to approach the age of the Bond babes, and whenever Pierce (age forty-five) would start to wrap one in his arms I wanted to leap up and say, "Hey, get away from her, she's got a father out there, you know. Kiss someone your own age." Second, I picked up, during the opening chase sequence that is the best in Bond history, some driving tips.

I put them to good use that night. I ripped the driver's door open, jumped in, revved the engine, engaged the gears, and was off in a shower of snow and ice. At least I should have been. My wheels spun, and snow flew. But the car remained stubbornly in place. Trying not to scream with frustration, I shifted gears and attempted to rock the car out of the snowbank. No luck.

An older couple walking their dog stopped to witness my struggles. They looked fit and hearty to me. A little light exercise was just what the doctor had ordered.

"Quick," I yelled through the open window. "Urgent matter; please give me a push."

They got behind the car and shoved with all their might. Back and forth we went until finally, with a giant sucking sound, the car broke free. It was a shame that I showered the helpful seniors head to toe with salty slush, but sacrifices had to be made. I honked and waved cheerily to them as I tore into the streets.

There is an inviolable rule in life that, the greater your hurry, the more vital your appointment, the more red lights you get. Indeed, a sea of red awaited me. Time was marching magisterially on, and there was nothing I could do about it. I swung into the side streets, trying to take a short cut. It worked wonderfully until I got stuck behind a snowplough. I deked around a corner, sped down the block, and turned back — just in time to find myself right back behind the plough.

I envied James Bond at that moment. He would have driven over the sidewalks and across a few lawns, gliding in front of that plough in a heartbeat. I thought about it, but sanity prevailed. I admitted defeat as the drive continued with red lights, snow-ploughs, pedestrians using crosswalks, and drivers cruising slowly to enjoy the Christmas lights. I pulled up at the church and sadly slunk inside to face a disappointed daughter.

"Great timing," my wife whispered to me as I sank into my seat. "The concert started late. You just made it."

I had forgotten the ultimate Christmas concert rule: nothing ever starts on time. Elizabeth and her compatriots climbed onstage, and she showered me with a smile that made it all worthwhile. Triple dad points awarded, plus a gold star. I wouldn't have missed it for the world. Those little girls and that one brave boy sang their hearts out. Brava and bravo.

Over the years, I have accumulated a deep and profound wisdom on how to survive your children's or grandchildren's elementary school Christmas concert. The key to the whole event is seating. Let's face it, if you are standing at the back of the gym, up against the wall, the delight and pride of your life will be but a vague blob in the distance, and you may wind up waving madly to someone else's child because you cannot find your own. So get there early. Some experts would advise forty-five to sixty minutes before the start time. Rookies making rookie mistakes. At the forty-five-minute mark, the place is packed, and parents are pillaging class-rooms looking for extra chairs. At the thirty-minute mark, even the principal's chair isn't safe.

No, the only way to guarantee that perfect seat is

to grab your place the day before or just after breakfast on game day at the absolute latest. Granted, you and the other parents will have to duck during volleyball practice or use your chair as a shield during gym time when the kids play dodge ball. But the occasional contusion will be well worth it by nightfall. Yes, you and yours will be not more than twenty rows back when the music starts.

Always aim for an aisle seat. That way, even if the person in front of you is six foot seven, you can still see. More importantly, when your child's class comes onstage, you won't be crushed by parents rushing to the aisle to take pictures . . . because you'll get there first. Where their children are involved, normally sane and balanced adults such as me are transformed into a foaming media scrum. I myself have a wonderful collection of school concert photographs, and, if I put the pictures under an electron microscope, I can just pick out my daughters.

There may be some parents with younger children out there who are thinking to themselves, "After my child sings, I'm out of here." Bad, very bad. It's rude to the other children, not to mention distracting to everyone else when you crawl over 450 people to get to the door. But, my friends, the organizers are ahead of you — way, way ahead of you. You think it is a coincidence that the kindergarten children are always just about last on the program?

Yes, I have seen faces fall when that realization sets in. So sit back and enjoy, and bring snacks for the preschool set. We don't mind being cascaded with Cheerios or catching the odd bottle that a distracted eighteen month old tosses out. We'll make way so they can go for walks. We're happy to help; we're parents too.

Cheer loudly, especially for the grade seven band. It is an act of musical courage. Greater love hath no parents than to smile supportively when one of their progeny arrives home in September carrying a tuba. These artists start off with three lone notes and by mid-December can produce a rendition of "Jingle Bells" that is almost recognizable. They squeak, they squawk, they wheeze. They possess boldness, if not accuracy.

There are certain events you can count on during this evening. The kindergarten children will touch your heart: they are so excited; you are so proud. They peer through the lights, seeking the faces of their parents, and then wave wildly when they find them. It doesn't matter what they sing; it's all wonderful. All the kids, from the resident comics and the academics to the children with regular meeting times at the principal's office, do their best. They realize this evening is special and give it their all. You'll hear the favourites — "Rudolph," "Frosty," "The Huron Carol," "Deck the Halls" — and a new favourite, "High Tech Santa":

*Santa's got a pager, and he's got a cell phone
too; just enter in the number, and he'll get
right back to you. This Christmas when
you've made your list of things you hope to
get, turn on your home computer and just
use the Internet. Santa dot com dot North
Pole's the secret phrase to use. He's also got
a fax machine, if that is the route you choose.*[1]

But there will also be skits with elves and kids
dressed as Christmas trees, choirs of all descriptions,
and teachers encouraging and leading their charges.

Having survived the school concert, we barely got to
take a breath before we had to plunge ourselves into
the nail-biting tension of Elizabeth's first real skating
competition.

A few years ago, we enrolled both Sarah and
Elizabeth in the CanSkate program so they could
learn to skate well. Sarah, my ballet daughter, toler-
ated the sessions and was quite happy to stop after a
year. But not my Elizabeth. No, my Elizabeth loved
it, so the next year we returned, and her skills
improved. We had joined Canada's frozen fraternity

[1]"High Tech Santa," lyrics by Angela Darter Stogsdill, music by Cristi
Miller. Hal Leonard, Milwaukee, 1997. Used with permission.

of ice parents, all to be found huddling for warmth around their coffees and hot chocolates in cold arenas on Saturday mornings — early, early Saturday mornings — while watching their children skate or play hockey. This is a deep and abiding part of Canadian parenting and a civic tradition. While some cultures offer airy piazzas, outdoor cafés, and town squares where people gather, we offer ice rinks and doughnut shops. These are the two places in our community where, if I sit long enough, I will meet every member of my congregation. Caffeine in cardboard cups and sugar-drenched carbohydrates are Canada's gift to the world.

As part of the CanSkate experience, I noticed that some kids spent a couple of minutes one on one with a coach at the end of each session. "Hmm," I thought to myself, "that could benefit Lizzy. She started later than most. I'm sure it couldn't cost us that much. . . ." If you listen very closely, you can hear the sound of skating parents laughing hysterically as they read that comment.

I polled a couple of parents, and the consensus was that a woman named Monica would be a good fit for Lizzy. We retained her services for ten minutes a week and saw our daughter improve immediately. That spring, to conclude the session, the club had an internal competition. Elizabeth came away with a silver medal in one event. I have never seen my daughter glow with such pride. She wore that medal around the house. It was beside her bed, on her desk. It was a true symbol of accomplishment for her. One that sealed our fate, for we were now officially a skating family.

The next fall she catapulted into what is known as Level 1. We appeared at the rink early that September. Liz in her jeans and her Canadian Tire skates was faced with girls whizzing around the ice in tights and dresses, sporting skates whose cost were beyond my most alarming nightmare.

Monica told us that Lizzy's skates wouldn't give her the support necessary for the jumps and spins she was about to learn. I was then informed that a skate exchange was to be held the next week, where we could acquire a pair of used figure skates.

I arrived the following Saturday with Elizabeth in tow to discover a crowd of excited skating parents clustered around tables waiting for the skates to appear. A mother immediately pulled me aside and informed me that she had a pair of skates available for a mere four hundred dollars! They were barely used. Her daughter, she informed me feverishly, had grown out of them in just over two months. I smiled gently, removed her hand, which was clamped to my forearm, and walked toward the tables.

The skates appeared, and the parents descended upon them in a feeding frenzy. I had absolutely no idea what to look for in a figure skate, so I just grabbed three pairs in Elizabeth's size and found a place to sit. There are times in life when you have to make a choice. Either you pretend you know what you are doing, bluff it out, and hope for the best, or you be a man, admit the truth, and beg for help. I begged. My pleas were heard, and a classmate of Wendy's from teachers' college (see *Annus horribilis*) appeared at my side. She inspected the skates, cast aside two pairs, and approved the third.

Indeed, they did fit Elizabeth (with growing room), so we headed over to ice pad two, to get Monica's seal of approval. My helper explained that, in order to get them sharpened properly, I had to book an appointment with a specialist sharpener in Oshawa — he and only he could guarantee the proper edge. This was said with the reverence usually reserved for neurosurgeons or reliable mechanics. Book an appointment to sharpen a pair of skates? Clearly, I was entering a parallel universe. We left the arena that day with skates, tights, and a purple skating costume. We were set.

The next few months were a whirlwind of waltz jumps and toe loops. I watched my daughter do things on the ice that I had seen before only on television. Admittedly, she was quite a distance from a triple flip, but it was fascinating to see her develop. She'd fall, get up, brush herself off, and try it again and again until she had mastered it. Her music for the one-and-a-half-minute routine was from the film *That's Entertainment* and from "Bring Him Home" from *Les Miserables*. Piece by piece, step by step, I watched a performance come together. I saw Lizzy skate solidly for two straight hours twice a week. In late November, she was, Monica informed us, ready to compete.

The competition was scheduled for a Sunday afternoon. So when church ended, we hurried home, and Elizabeth changed into the newly purchased purple performance dress with sequins. It whooshed and flowed in all the right places, and she felt like Michelle Kwan.

We arrived at the arena just after 1:00, surrounded by a multitude of small girls from all over eastern Ontario. The skaters and their parents were excited, and anticipation filled the air. Skating parents have quite a reputation, most of which is unwarranted. In any sport, you will come across the occasional over-anxious personality who sees every other child as a competitive threat and is overly generous with help-ful hints for the coach. Or you might run into the odd coach from the dark side of the force who believes that sheer loudness will increase the per-formance skills of her charges. But the vast majority of parents and coaches I have met in skating are encouraging and supportive toward their own children and all who are participating. Olympic gold medallists are not plentiful, so for most of us the thrill lies in watching our children do their best. Yet, I must confess, even I have been known to possibly, from infinitesimal time to infinitesimal time, make a slight, tiny, hardly noticeable, mild suggestion to my daughter when she is on the ice. But she just gives me this "Oh, Dad!" look and goes merrily on her way.

Liz was enrolled in the competition, given a dressing room number, and sent off to wait her turn. Sarah and I secured seats in the stands while Wendy helped Liz to get changed. I saw Monica in the distance, and then Wendy waved me over to tie Lizzy's skates.

This is not as simple as it sounds. Tying up figure skates is an art in itself and my one great skill. I may be a certified danger around power tools, but my gosh can I tie skates. The key is finding the delicate balance between the laces being just taut enough to support the foot and being so tight they cut off all circulation from the ankle down.

I laced up Lizzy's skates, checking each loop. Liz pulled, I pulled, we got it just right. I slapped each skate on both sides for luck, and she was off. As I walked back to my seat, a young man wearing a gold medal came through the door and said to his companion, "I'm going to sit with the peasants."

"Peasants?" I replied, arching an eyebrow. "We're parents, not peasants."

An additional witticism died on my lips as he looked right through me. Twenty minutes later, just before Liz went on the ice, I glanced over at the judging panel, and there he was, not just a skater but also a judge, gulp.

As I watched my youngest warm up, I could feel her adrenaline surging up from ice level. She went back to the door and waited with Monica, who was talking intently to her, gesturing, and making last-minute adjustments.

Finally, they announced Elizabeth's name. She came onto the ice with a big smile, her skirt swooshing. The music started, and she was off. For one minute and thirty seconds.

I was on the edge of my seat. Or I would have been if I was sitting. I was standing ramrod straight, feeling every move she made. All those countless hours, all that practice, leading up to this one minute and thirty seconds.

Arms up, she skated forward and into her program: bunny hop, look to the left with arms raised, bunny hop, look to the right, push forward, glide, two-foot spin followed by a back-and-forth shimmy, two crosscuts and a one-foot spin, four pushes forward with arms up, four backward crosscuts followed by the tricky waltz jump—toe loop combination. (I held my breath when she went up and breathed again when she nailed it perfectly.) Four forward pushes and an extended spiral, her strongest element. Another toe loop followed by four backward pushes with ballet arms extended. The mood shifts from the exuberance of the opening music to the "Bring Him Home" section. Five more backward pushes followed by a backward spiral. Three forward pushes into two glide spins. Two forward crosscuts and two arabesques, two more bunny hops, and the music returns to *That's Entertainment*. Four backward crosscuts and a waltz jump, then three backward crosscuts into a sit spin. More crosscuts and glides into a salchow jump, three more pushes and a drag, a one-foot spin, three steps to the left, leg extension, three to the right, leg extension, arms twirl up, big smile, and it's done.

She wobbled once or twice but receives a perfect score of 6.0 from us. The family goes nuts, and the rest of the audience demonstrates enthusiasm. Lizzy curtsies to the stands, then to the judges, and she's off the ice. She explodes into the arms of her coach, and both of them have smiles as wide as the rink.

While she attained a ribbon and not a medal, it was her first competition; she medalled for all of us and, most importantly, for herself.

At this point, we parents were becoming disoriented, unsure which event we were actually attending. But ballet was next, for both girls, and so we pressed on.

The dance studio is located on the second storey

of an old munitions factory built before the Second World War. It certainly has the appropriate Bohemian feel, with its wooden beams, exposed pipes and ceiling, and ductwork. We walked up two flights of stairs, past the pictures that the artist who shares the space has on display. I took off my boots and went beyond the table filled with Christmas crafts that the performing workshop group were selling to raise funds for their spring show, through the change area, and into the studio. The seats awaiting us were an odd collection from times gone by, and I gingerly lowered myself down into one. I well remembered the previous year, when I sat down and the chair, deciding that I had eaten enough pre-Christmas goodies, heaved a sigh of despair and gave way. I plummeted to the floor with my legs waving in the air. As a piece of choreography, it left a lot to be desired.

Sarah and the rest of the girls came in, warmed up, and then began. While not wallowing too deeply in nostalgia, I cast my mind back to when she was three years old and first started dancing. There she was, in a group of little girls all pretending to be raindrops. From the very beginning, she loved it: the discipline, the mental and physical challenges. Year after year she has gained knowledge and experience and changed from that little girl into a real dancer. But the big change happened when she started dancing on pointe. Imagine, if you will, slipping on a pair of canvas shoes that are glued and nailed together. There is no arch support, only a wood and leather insole, without a hint of padding. You put them on and stand up, not just on the flat of your feet, mind you, but also straight up on your toes, with all the weight of your body bearing down on them. Just for fun, you go for a walk and run across a stage. Ouch! Are your toes aching from the very thought of it? Are you seeing *The Nutcracker* ballet in a whole new light? Contrary to popular myth, when ballerinas put on pointe shoes, their toes are not cushioned in a thick foam.

Sarah, warming up, stretched, pliéd, and tendued. She lifted her foot up to the top of the barre and gracefully leaned forward, her nose touching her knee. (If I tried that, I would need to seek medical attention. I never bent that way, even at her age.) After more stretches, she danced across the floor, step after intricate step, laughing with her friends huddled in the corner. Then she strapped on the pointe shoes and lifted up onto her toes. Sarah made it look effortless. As she smiled over at us and lifted one leg, I could imagine her as a three-year-old child, watching her older self in amazement at what she would become.

Exhausted and ravenous from all this activity, we head home to the kitchen. It's time for some Christmas cooking.

On the Eighth Day before Christmas,

my true loves gave to me

eight Christmas cookies in the shape

of an enormous pine tree.

There are now eight days to go. That means family parties to plan for and, of course, that climactic meal, the Christmas dinner, to organize. Hundreds of shoppers are jammed together in the supermarket, working through long lists of Yuletide provisions. The grocery store attempts to calm our frazzled nerves with piped-in Christmas carols and cashiers in red elf hats. Traffic is heavy, and on aisle three there is a pileup — a loading bin filled with plum puddings is slowing traffic. Carts are backed up around the dairy case and into the freezer section. As people search for alternative routes, all the other aisles fill up. Carts attempting to pass in both directions are caught between people looking for that one item on the shelves they cannot find.

Frustration builds, stress levels increase, and total store gridlock is but moments away when a flying squad of stackers clears the bin and pushes it to the back of the store. Slowly, the backup eases, and traffic returns to near normal. Customers waiting in cashier lineups are munching their groceries, reading magazines, placating children, and generally acting as though they are on a camp-out. I go from aisle to aisle, making my list and checking it twice.

If this were a typical shopping trip, my cart

would be a perfect example of healthy eating according to Canada's Food Guide: fruits, vegetables, whole-grain bread, and skinless chicken breasts. Even those two perky *Body Break* types would beam their approval. But today they would gaze at me mournfully. For piled high in my cart are brie, whipping cream, pâté, butter, baked goods, and so many other forbidden items that a dietician could have the cart impounded as a public health hazard. But it gets worse, much, much worse.

As I pass the dairy case, purchasing my one healthy product, skim milk, I see the ultimate in forbidden Christmas fruit: eggnog. A carton of full-fat, full-calorie, tempting, delicious eggnog. My Christmas-time downfall lies before me. I pick it up, listening to its siren call: "Drink me, drink me." I shake it a bit to hear that enticing slosh of eggs, mixed with whole milk, sugar, cinnamon, nutmeg, and enough additives to preserve the pharaohs. Other cartons of "fat-free" or "fat-reduced" nog are nestled up beside the real thing. I ignore them. They have no appeal. Casting a guilt-ridden glance around me, I slip the nog underneath two heads of lettuce and head for the checkout counter.

The shame: this is neither the first nor the last carton of the season. Ah, the taste of that first glass as the nog slips down the throat like a guilty secret. Yum, yum, yum. But then it never stops at just one, oh no. If I'm not careful, I'll drink so much of the stuff that I'll look like Friar Tuck by Christmas Eve, with my stomach arriving at the front of the church five minutes before the rest of me catches up. It takes all my iron will to ration myself to one small glass a day.

For some unexplained reason, only supermarket eggnog will do. I have been plied with homemade concoctions prepared with real cream, and they are very good. But for me eggnog must come from a carton. There are some fellow aficionados who believe that the addition of rum to the nog is an absolute necessity. While I have been known to combine the two for strictly medicinal purposes, such as fighting off the billions of cold germs that are flying around at this time of year, I don't really believe in anything that could possibly dilute the sugar. Once the rest of the family spot that first container, it is a battle to preserve my share. Except for Sarah. She's allergic to eggs and all dairy products. As the resident chef, I have spent years attempting to produce an acceptable homemade rice milk ricenog. I have experimented with honey, corn syrup, brown sugar, and the appropriate spices to provide a drink that has a similar texture and taste to ours. Modestly, I admit success, and Sarah Nog vanishes as fast as I can make it.

Fortunately, my other great passion at this season is not so deadly to the waistline: mandarin oranges. These I inhale by the case. There is something so wonderful about the way the peel falls off and the small sections break apart. Give me an armful of mandarins with eggnog chasers, and I'm a happy man.

Well, just about. For the complete pre-Christmas snack, a couple of cookies need to be added to the mix: homemade Christmas cookies shaped like reindeer, angels, bells, holly, and Christmas trees. Wendy and the girls bake them each year. The kitchen is covered in flour and pastry as my daughters roll out the dough at the table, discuss the merits of adding multicoloured sugar sprinkles (I vote no but am overruled except for one batch), and vie for the honour of putting the first tray in the oven. Nutmeg and cinnamon combine with oatmeal in a cookie recipe that goes back generations in my family. It has the added advantage for those with allergies in that it is both egg and dairy free. Every bite takes me back to my childhood and to early marriage, when my daughters were very young. In those years, the whole process could take a full day, with tiny figures wearing aprons and little fingers surreptitiously stuffing dough into their mouths. The cookies often appeared in uncertain and unique shapes, with reindeer resembling hippos, for example, but their enthusiasm more than compensated for any culinary imperfections.

If you seek a wonderful Christmas cookie, and a memorable family moment, here's a recipe that comes from my grandmother.

Crisp Oatmeal Cookies
Makes about 16 cookies

2 cups pastry flour
2 cups rolled oats
1 cup sugar
½ cup shortening
½ cup rice milk*
½ tsp vanilla
½ tsp baking soda
¼ tsp nutmeg
¼ tsp salt

Combine ingredients into a ball. Chill, preferably overnight. Roll thin, cut out into appropriate Xmas shapes, and bake at 350° F (180° C) for 10 minutes. Double the recipe and hide some because they disappear faster than they can be made.

* We use rice milk, but soy will do or the dairy variety if you choose.

What is it, I wonder, about Christmas and food? The two have been inextricably linked for centuries. Who has ever gone to a Christmas party without sampling delicacy after delicacy? After all, it would be rude to the hosts not to partake of their generous offerings. When Charles Dickens talked about how "abundance rejoices" during the Christmas season, he knew of which he spoke.

That certainly proves to be the case when we host our Yuletide family party. This is a yearly tradition in our house, a way of gathering the family to welcome my sister home on her Christmas visit. Holding a family party before Christmas is, of course, an act of calculated insanity. But there are some tips I have gleaned over the years: (1) do no cooking yourselves — buy only frozen; our choice is lasagne: meat, vegetarian, and sometimes seafood; (2) get everybody to bring something.

The latter approach requires strategic thinking. Who makes a good salad; whose desserts are second to none; who has a flair for hors d'oeuvres; who can be counted on to bring wine? Who always arrives late? Who is early? There is no point assigning hors d'oeuvres to the person who always arrives sixty minutes after the start time. But when it comes to the food, all of us here know what happens: the salads are from a bag, the hors d'oeuvres require defrosting, and the desserts come in a cardboard package. It's a week before Christmas. Who has time for anything else?

But it doesn't matter. My family (on my father's side) is coming over. That means thirty of my nearest and dearest are descending en masse: uncles, aunts, cousins of the first and second variety. Three generations, all those I love.

I'm ecstatic because I love a crowd, always have, always will. This trend started when I was still quite young. I was four years old, and we were living in London, England, when my sister had her first birthday. My parents had made some arrangements to celebrate what I considered to be a monumental event. But in my view, these arrangements were inadequate. They lacked vision — in particular, they lacked sufficient resources in people. So, knowing that in their hearts they wanted me to correct what they themselves would have had to admit was an egregious error, I proceeded to go door to door and invite absolutely everyone in our apartment building to the party. I don't remember the precise phrases used by my parents as their flat kept filling with people, some of whom they had never met before. But from my perspective, the first anniversary of my sibling's birth was being appropriately celebrated.

Ever since then, I have been happiest surrounded by people, either at home or at church. So a family Christmas party finds me in my natural element. It's not that hard to get the house ready with a quick vacuum, a light dusting, all the junk stuffed into one of the bedrooms, nailing that room's door shut . . . and then it's just stand back and enjoy the fun. Open the front door as wave upon wave of relatives pour in. There's my father over in the corner, engaged in an intense discussion on politics with my cousin's husband. My sister and uncle are talking about her business. My cousin's son, Adam, is trying his long line of jokes on my other cousin, Kevin, who is a stand-up comic and a writer. The new moms are comparing baby tips, and I'm trying to keep the toddlers from eating the Christmas tree.

Downstairs in the family room, the teenagers are updating e-mail addresses, playing Twister or cards, and attempting to figure out exactly how they are related to each other. Are they first cousins, second cousins once removed, or third cousins removed by force? The kitchen is packed with people; the house is alive with conversation. Corks are popping, and punch is being poured. The food you were sure would feed an army disappears as people eat standing up or with plates perched precariously on their laps. The occasional spill is inevitable, but hardly a cause for concern, and sooner or later a toddler makes it through my gauntlet of chairs to rearrange the tree. Camera flashes go off as various relatives record the event for posterity.

In the middle of it all, Wendy and I clear plates, lay out more food, and make sure that our guests have all they need. Stories are shared of growing up together, memories rekindled, family ties strengthened. Before you know it, dessert is served. Coffee and tea make the rounds, and the guests regretfully begin to make their departures. We collapse on the couch, exhausted, the house and us looking a little worse for wear. But we are filled with that weary contentment that comes from a truly wonderful evening.

Every family has its own traditions around the food served. Take mine, for instance. While some families have a Christmas Eve tradition involving food such as tourtière, that wonderful French Canadian meat pie, I spend that evening at church with the cast and crew of our Christmas Eve play. Which explains why my Christmas Eve culinary tradition consists of pizza and pop, followed by a box of Timbits, with about twenty-five teenagers and ten adults in a church basement. Nothing says Christmas to me like double cheese, pepperoni, and mushrooms.

But the food in and of itself is not what's really important; it's the meaning behind the food. For every family recipe is a story. A story of the family and its history, a treasure of memories that goes back to when we were all children and the world was filled with mystery and excitement.

Take, for example, my family's recipe for stuffing. I have tried every recipe known to humanity. I have peeled chestnuts till my fingers ached; I have tossed in seafood, spicy sausage, fruit, cornbread, and all manner of exotic ingredients. But no other stuffing, even if it comes from the most extraordinary of cordon bleu cookbooks, could ever approach my mom's recipe.

Before we go any further, let's agree on terms. The word is stuffing, not dressing. I was once commissioned by CBC Radio to do an in-depth report on this issue. After consulting countless volumes of cookbooks from all sides of the Atlantic, this is what I concluded: in

Canada and the United Kingdom, the proper term is stuffing. The United States, as evidenced by the bible of cooking sources, *The Joy of Cooking*, employs dressing to denote a side dish with poultry or game. For the rest of us, it's stuffing, as in we stuffed, he stuffed, they stuffed, we're stuffed.

Our stuffing has been passed down from time immemorial: from my great-grandmother, to her daughter, to my mom, and to me and my children. The ingredients are not particularly unusual: white bread, thyme, sage, salt, pepper, onions, and celery. The kicker, the rogue component that gives the stuffing its texture and transforms it into a mouth-watering taste explosion, is the humble potato, which when boiled and lightly mashed adds both body and depth to the concoction.

The paper bearing this recipe is stained with both Christmases and Thanksgivings past. My mom wrote it out for us a few years before she died. So I always talk about her to the girls when we cook the dinner. It's as if my mom is in the kitchen with us.

This sadder subplot works through the Christmases of many families. To be human is to experience loss. These losses ache more intensely when attention is focused on family and togetherness. At such times, we have a choice. Loss can overshadow the joy of Christmas, or the season can be an opportunity to remember with love and gratitude those no longer among us. This does not eliminate the pain, but it allows us to live with it and to recall what that person meant to us all.

Thus it is that Mom's stuffing recipe tells us who we were, who we are, and who we will become as a family. For layered upon the story of my mother are the stories of my girls. When the three of us start the process, past Christmases arise. "Do you remember the time when . . ." someone starts to say. One story flows into another and into another and into another. My sister, who has never missed a Christmas with us since Sarah was born, often stars in these stories. She is usually nearby as we work, helping to assemble the dinner. Wendy walks in and out, adding her versions of the various events, while Elizabeth indicates that, when she grows up and is out on her own, she has first dibs on the next Christmas dinner. She has been saying this since she was five years old, and that time is coming faster than I care to acknowledge.

Before we know it, the turkey is stuffed. We all gaze admiringly at it, professing that it is the best turkey we have ever seen. Sarah says thank you to the turkey for agreeing to join us for dinner (while acknowledging that it may not have been a totally voluntary decision). The bird is put in the oven, and within thirty minutes essence of gobbler begins to fill our home.

The best thing to do at some point on Christmas

Day is to get out of the house and go for a walk. This will accomplish a number of things. You will get exercise, which, after all you have eaten and are about to eat, is an absolute necessity. The fresh air will clear the fuzziness that comes from being awakened at the crack of dawn. But the real reason is so that you can walk back into your home with your olfactory and gustatory senses totally clear. Ah, the fragrance of cooking turkey. What an experience! Food and emotion all rolled into one.

So here, without further ado, is my mom's stuffing recipe. May it grace your table with the joy it gives ours.

Jane White's Turkey Stuffing
Amounts by guess or by golly, for a 12-pound turkey.
Amounts are approximate — change to taste.

1 ½ cups cool cooked mashed potatoes
1 loaf (approx.) sliced white bread broken
   into 1-1 ½" pieces
1 ½ cups chopped onion
1 cup chopped celery
4 tbsp bacon fat*
¼ cup chopped parsley
1 ½ tbsp sage
1 tsp thyme
1 tsp marjoram
2 tsp salt, I think; start with a little taste
pepper to taste

Sauté onions and celery in bacon fat till limp in frying pan.
Let cool for handling. Combine all ingredients with your

hands. The mixture should form and hold a ball easily and have a slightly moist consistency. Keep the potato water and use it to moisten the mix if it is too dry.

* 1 tbsp margarine is just fine instead of the bacon fat, but the bacon fat does give the best flavour.

My mom absolutely adored everything about Christmas. Mom would be humming carols by early November, but Christmas dinner is what she loved the most. When we were older, this dinner would start off with raw oysters followed by the main event, the turkey, followed by the traditional plum pudding. Mom was a bit nearsighted, which led to the Christmas when she almost torched the house.

It was an El Niño Christmas, back in the 1980s, in the era we refer to as BC, or Before Children. The weather was appalling. Instead of being twenty below with snow on the ground, as required by all self-respecting Canadian Christmases, it was a balmy fifteen degrees Celsius. We had our jackets and ties off and shirtsleeves rolled up. It was late in the evening when Mom brought out the pudding. She had placed a holly wreath on top for decoration. Mom applied the brandy to her pudding with enthusiasm. She then lit the match and touched it to the dessert. What she did not realize was that she was still pouring the liquor when she applied the match. The result was a Christmas dessert that was more

Molotov cocktail than plum pudding.

"Mom," we cried out in unison, "watch out — the whole plate's on fire!"

She didn't have her glasses on and didn't believe us. So she kept pouring on the brandy as the bonfire grew in intensity. I dashed to the kitchen to grab the fire extinguisher while calculating how long it would take for the fire department to arrive and whether I would have time to get my presents out first. Mom finally caught on when the holly on top of the pudding burst into flames and the berries popped like corn in a microwave. Eventually, the blaze died down, and the fire extinguisher was not needed. Inexplicably, my mother looked at the pudding, saw that the flames were almost out, and poured on more brandy. . . . Whoosh, one carbonized plum pudding, complemented by the fragrance of smoked holly.

But let's be brutally honest. Does anyone actually like Christmas pudding? Here I refer to the tinned variety as opposed to the kind lovingly created from scratch. I mean, really, after the turkey, the yams, the mashed potatoes, the Brussels sprouts (yuck, says my sister), the corn, and the cranberry sauce, who really wants a dessert that could be used as ballast on a sailing ship?

It's really the hard sauce that people like. It's that combination of butter, brandy, and icing sugar that's irresistible. Check out the balance of sauce to pudding on your family members' forks, and you'll see that sauce wins hands down.

But I have an alternative for you, introduced to me by Wendy. This is an option created by my mother-in-law of Scottish descent: carrot pudding. This is not carrot cake, covered in nuts and cream cheese icing, but a steamed pudding that is light (no suet) and graced with an absolutely delicious brown sugar sauce. The perfect end to the perfect meal, with the bonus that your smoke detector won't erupt when it's being served. But feel free to douse it with brandy and set it alight; just keep in mind that generations of my in-laws, all fine Scottish teetotalling Presbyterians, will be staring at you when you do!

So here is Agnes Hedder-wick's famous carrot pudding with brown sugar sauce.

Carrot Pudding, Steamed

Serves 6

1 cup raisins
½ cup currants
½ cup butter or margarine, softened
1 cup grated carrots
1 cup grated raw potatoes
1 cup all-purpose flour
1 tsp baking powder
1 tsp cinnamon
½ tsp salt
½ tsp ground nutmeg
¼ tsp ground cloves

Put raisins and currants in a small bowl. Cover with 1/2 cup boiling water; let stand 5 minutes. Drain well; set aside. In a large bowl, beat butter or margarine with sugar until light and fluffy. Stir in carrots, potatoes, raisins, and currants until well mixed.

In a separate bowl, combine flour, baking soda, and seasoning. Stir into carrot mixture until well moistened. Spoon batter into greased pudding mould or heat-proof bowl. Cover tightly with lid or foil tied with string. Place on rack in deep saucepan or preserving kettle. Pour boiling water into saucepan to reach halfway up sides of mould. Cover and steam, occasionally adding boiling water to retain water level, for three hours or until toothpick comes out cleanly.

Brown Sugar Sauce*

½ cup brown sugar
1 tbsp flour
1 cup boiling water
1 tbsp butter or margarine
1 tsp vanilla
¼ tsp salt

Mix together brown sugar, flour, and salt in a saucepan. Add boiling water slowly; cook and stir over direct heat till smooth and slightly thickened. Simmer for five minutes. Remove from heat and add margarine or butter and vanilla. Stir until dissolved; serve hot.

* I always double this recipe in order to have plenty of sauce.

But now the parties are over, and I begin to dream of the ultimate Christmas food experience, Christmas breakfast and dinner, one week hence.

On the subject of Christmas breakfast, Wendy and I come from two very different traditions. Her family grazed as they opened gifts, while mine had to sit down at the table before opening gifts. My mom's dad was a doctor who subscribed to the medical belief that breakfast was, in fact, the most important meal of the day, especially Christmas Day. Upon rising, we were allowed to open our stockings, but, just when the presents were crying out to be descended upon and ripped open, we had to troop into the dining room for breakfast.

When I say breakfast, I mean a full and complete breakfast, no quick bowl of cornflakes gulped down at high speed. Oh no, bacon, eggs, toast, and then coffee for the adults. Only after the last sip of coffee were we allowed back into the living room to open the presents. Let me tell you that that breakfast added a whole new meaning to the space-time continuum. Every mouthful seemed to take an hour; every sip of coffee was an eternity. So when I married and had children, that was one family tradition I happily discarded.

As a compromise, our family opens its gifts with tea and Chelsea buns. Not just any Chelsea buns but the finest, the stickiest, the Chelsiest buns in all of creation. Buns that taste not of winter but of summer. To get these buns, you have to drive far and long to a quiet highway near our family cottage. There, by the side of the road, marked by a gas company sign, sits an old house that functions as a general store. They have everything: fishing tackle, coal-oil lamps, groceries, a post office, ice cream, candy, and dew worms for fishing. Behind the front counter lies a baking case. In that case resides an ambrosia of baked goods: pies, butter tarts, and bread. But their greatest triumph is their homemade Chelsea buns. These are simply carbohydrate poetry, with their drippings of brown sugar, raisins, and cinnamon. In fact, to add that touch of authenticity, to double-check my sources, and to make sure that I am one hundred percent accurate in my descriptions, I'm eating some right now. Bliss.

On the Seventh Day before Christmas,

I gathered by my side

seven favourite stories to read under

the enormous pine tree.

In the corner of the living room, beside the piano, sits the big red wing chair. We bought it in the early years of our marriage, when we could barely afford the mortgage payments on our new home. But when I saw it sitting in the store in the strip mall, I knew it was special. It looked like the type of chair that would invite you to sink comfortably into its depths with a good book on a snowy winter's day, the kind of chair your children would climb up on to sit in your lap for story time.

That is exactly what that chair has been for our family. It is the focal point of our seating arrangements. Guests immediately head for that spot, and when my father-in-law is visiting it's a sprint between the two of us to see who will get there first. Subterfuge and cunning have been used to entice the current occupant to vacate the chair for an instant, whereupon it is seized and laid claim to. How far have things gone? You be the judge.

I arrived home after a long day to find Sarah comfortably ensconced in my favourite seat. My entreaties that, as the senior member of the firm, I should have priority were rejected. "Sarah," I said in my most fatherly voice, "it's my chair, it's my turn." The irrefutable logic of my argument was ignored.

Clearly, some nefarious scheming was required. What could I do to entice her off the chair? Bribery? It would never work. Threats of a lifetime grounding? Hollow, and she knew it. What, I wondered, was the weak spot that could be strategically exploited to my advantage? It came to me in a blinding flash. I slipped upstairs to my bedroom, pulled out my cell-phone, and called our home number.

The phone rang. "Sarah," I called out. "Could you get the phone?" I watched from the bedroom door as she got up and walked into the kitchen. I ran down-stairs at a gallop and sat down just as she picked up the phone.

"Hello, Sarah White speaking," she answered politely.

"Hi, Sarah, it's Dad," I said. "How are you?"

Silence. Then, "Dad, what are you doing?"

"Oh, just calling you on the cellphone to say hi."

Silence again, followed by a puzzled voice. "Where are you?"

"Me?" I responded in an off-the-cuff tone. "In the living room, sitting in the red wing chair."

I heard a scream. The phone crashed down, and an outraged teenager came steaming around the corner. A cannonball is the term used to describe a leap off the dock into the water. Height and distance are the goals of this particular manoeuvre. I had never before been the target of one while sitting in my house, but I was in the moments following my oh-so-clever idea. While I was temporarily successful in reclaiming the chair, I placed that particular move into the bulging file known as "It seemed like a good idea at the time."

Across the room from the red chair, on the floor beside the couch, sits a wooden magazine rack, filled to the brim with Christmas stories. Modern and historical, written for both adults and children. It stays there all through the year. From time to time, no matter what the season, one of the family will stop, reach over, pull out one of the books, and take time to read a few pages. Come November, each of the books is taken out and read one by one. Every one of these volumes not only tells its own story but also has a tale attached to it. Where it was purchased, the time in our lives, the memories associated with its first reading — these factors are as important as the stories themselves.

As I look at the contents of that rack spread out across the floor, it is the sheer variety that amazes me. *The Night before Christmas* by Clement C. Moore, that most famous of poems, has captivated generations of children and given us our modern Santa Claus. Moore is said to have written it on Christmas Eve for his children, while others have him writing it after a sleigh ride, basing the character of Saint Nick on the sleigh driver. Some say that he wrote it entirely him-self. Others say that he drew on previously published works and was deeply influenced by the Dutch ver-sion of Father Christmas, Sinter Klaus. Whatever the case, the tall, thin saint who before this could be quite dour while delivering presents was transformed forever into "a right jolly old elf." Wendy purchased our particular edition not for the girls but for me! The illustrations are by Greg and Tim Hildebrandt, whose *Lord of the Rings* calendars were on my walls all through university.

When I want to get in the Christmas mood, I automatically pull out a small book called *Christmas: A Treasury of Verse and Prose*, edited by Sheila Pickles. This is a delightful buffet of excerpts from all the Christmas classics from the nineteenth and early twentieth centuries. Illustrated with beautifully coloured plates, it always gives me that sense of being part of a long history of celebrating this season. Fifteen minutes of scanning this treasure trove can add balance to any harried December day.

We got that book and many others from a won-derful bookstore in southwest Calgary. The store was not huge but carried everything we wanted. It was there that we found Brian Wildsmith's book *A Christmas Story*. We were captured by it because the main character was a girl named Rebecca who fol-lows Mary and Joseph in search of the donkey who bears them because she hopes to reunite the donkey with its foal. With two daughters in our home, we were always on the lookout for Christmas stories with heroines.

When we lived in Springbank, Alberta, my day off was one of our favourite times. Instead of packing up the car and heading for the mountains, we would put Sarah in the back seat and drive into Calgary, where we could experience the glories of sidewalks, traffic, restaurants, and malls. In particular, we would haunt bookstores, spending our time looking through the shelves for just the right purchase. Once, in the heart of downtown, we wandered into a bookstore and immediately felt that we had entered 84 Charing Cross Road, that book retailer in London, England, made famous by Helene Hanff's book of the same name. Gleaming dark wood, high shelves with a railing on top to support the ladder that staff would move around to shelve and bring down books.

The store's hushed atmosphere was coupled with a radical innovation: a coffee bar. We spent many a happy afternoon there wandering the aisles, drinking coffee, getting books for Sarah and for ourselves. We credit Sarah's love of reading to those afternoons. To her, reading is like breathing; she simply inhales books.

It was while wandering through that Calgary store that we discovered my all-time favourite children's book, *Christmas!* by the brilliant illustrator Peter Spier. What makes this book both unique and wonderful is its lack of text. Instead, it follows a family in pictures alone, working their way through the Christmas season. Shopping, decorating the house, baking, going to church on Christmas Eve, the dinner, the cleanup, and the packing up of all the decorations. We loved this book so much that we made our own version, taking photographs of our traditions and placing them in a photo album so that they matched the placement of the photos in the book. This and "The Night before Christmas" have the distinct honour of being the works that are read to the girls before bed every Christmas Eve.

We have other favourites that are well worth reading for children of all ages. In no particular order, I recommend the following.

My Prairie Christmas, by Brett Harvey. When we were in Alberta, we identified with this transplanted family's first Christmas in the west.

The Wild Christmas Reindeer, by Jan Brett. Everyone should have one of Jan's books; the illustrations alone are breathtaking.

Flight of the Reindeer: The True Story of Santa Claus and His Christmas Mission, by Robert Sullivan. For sheer whimsy, nothing quite matches this documentary stylebook on how reindeer fly.

The Christmas Miracle of Jonathan Toomey, an absolute classic by Susan Wojciechowski. This is a story of the power of a small boy to bring hope into the life of a man who has suffered the greatest loss any of us could face.

The Story of Christmas, written and illustrated by Jane Ray. This classic tells the biblical story of Jesus' birth, with glowing pictures that evoke a feel of Central America.

In December 1988, before Sarah was a year old, we were given a great book, written by Chris Van Allsburg. *The Polar Express* is filled with childlike wonder and real poignancy. It poses an important question to all adults: "Can you still experience Christmas, or have you lost the ability to truly see what is around you?" The inscription in the front reads

To Christopher, Wendy and Sarah,
May you always hear the Christmas bell ring!
Love,
Sheri, Jennie and Kristen

It has been just over a decade since I last saw Sheri and her two daughters. I would like her to know that all of us can still hear the bell, and I hope we always will.

Any of us who have had small children know that one book will catch their fancy for weeks on end. They want it read to them constantly. For Elizabeth, that book was *Twinkle, Twinkle, Little Star*, a Christmas version of the famous poem, illustrated by Julia Noonan. Lizzy received it in 1992, when she was almost two years old. It was our constant companion. She would wander into our bedroom in the morning, climb in between the two of us, and call out in an imperious sort of way, "kinkle, kinkle." She would not settle until we had regained consciousness sufficiently to read it to her. At breakfast, up into our laps she'd crawl or onto the couch when we were watching television. In the middle of the night, if she awoke, "kinkle, kinkle" would be the cry. I started repeating each page in my sleep. Anyone who walked into our house during that time was fair "kinkle, kinkle" game. My two favourite photographs from that period are of Lizzy holding up the book to my father, his face filled with laughter, and of him reading the book with Liz ensconced on his lap.

What would Christmas be without stories? The original one, of course, with shepherds, angels, and a stable is the foundation of all the others. But what a wealth has sprung from it! Who can imagine Christmas without Ebenezer Scrooge, the Grinch, Charlie Brown's tree, *The Night before Christmas*, the O. Henry story "The Gift of the Magi"? Each of these writers has found new ways to communicate the truth and beauty of this season.

My favourite of them all is Dickens's masterpiece *A Christmas Carol*. Written in just six weeks between October and November 1843, it was an instant classic when it was first published, selling six thousand copies in its first few days. Within two months, eight stage versions had sprung up across London, and before long it was winging its way to America. It has lasted as a story because, while it is set in a time far from our own, it is set in a time just like our own. The themes of greed, avarice, poverty, isolation, a child's illness, and redemption are universal and utterly human, no matter what the century.

Recently, while doing research for an Advent sermon series, I came upon two stories that, while very old, are new to me. They caught my imagination, and I have created my own versions of these ancient tales.

The songbird was tired, exhausted after weeks of flying. It was night. She should have found shelter hours ago, but on she flew, the light of a bright star guiding her way. She circled the town, which was crowded with people. Torches and lanterns illuminated the busy streets. The sounds of people selling goods and others seeking shelter filled the night air.

This night was different from all the others she had known. Usually, towns were quiet after sundown, their inhabitants' doors closed against the uncertainty of the dark. It was only then that she would feel safe to land. But not tonight. Tonight she felt only disquiet. She swooped down lower, trying to find a tree with some cover or an overhanging eve on a roof. Nothing. The bushes and trees were too close to the cacophony of the crowd for her to feel secure.

The songbird flew on to the edge of the village, passed an inn, and went through the yard and into the stable. There was light there and animals and straw, which meant food. She would have to be careful; there was bound to be a cat or two about. Caution would be her watchword. Her small brown body swept up and landed on a rafter in the stable's roof. There below her were the usual animals: a cow, a donkey, a few goats. But something else. Three humans: one newborn lying in a manger, a mother worn out and drawn, a troubled man. He was talking softly and urgently to the woman. Food, water, the need for another woman to help care for them all. He was reassuring but obviously concerned. With a look that was both proud and deeply worried, he slipped out into the night.

By the baby and the mother was a small fire. The woman gathered the child to her breast and sat by its fading heat. The woman was cold, and there was only a little fuel. The little bird looked at the child. He was different somehow from the other children she had seen on her travels, but she was unsure what made him so. She felt both thrill and unease.

The fire began to die. The songbird knew with a certainty that warmth was crucial for the survival of this small family. But what could she do, small as she was? She looked at the other animals and swooped over to the cow.

"Your breath, my friend, your deep, powerful breath would stir the fire; will you not rise and help?"

The cow thought about it for a time but said, "All my days people have wanted something from me. Tonight I cannot help."

The bird asked the donkey. Sadly, he was too tired after his long journey, bearing the burden of the woman and her tiny family. He had no breath left to give. The goats, too, protested. They would love to help, but what could they accomplish, small goats that they were? If the cow and the donkey would not give aid, then what business was it of the goats, or this visiting bird, for that matter? People and animals were best left separate, to their own devices. It would not do to have them mix.

The songbird was desperate. The fire was dying down to coals, the man had not returned, and the baby needed warmth. With an eye out for cats, the small brown figure flew down in front of the fire and beat her wings. The flames, dormant in the coals, sprang to life. She kept beating her wings, harder and harder, and the fire grew in its intensity. The woman, still tired, threw some more wood from the pile left beside her. The flames crackled and danced, and warmth once again filled the small barn.

There was a crack, and a tiny coal from a log flew across the firepit and onto the breast of the bird, still flapping her wings. Her breast was singed red from the spark, and it did not fade. It was a red that stayed with her all the days of her life and has lived in every generation of her kind from that day forward.

Thus it was that on Christmas Eve God blessed the robin for her generosity and gave her a red breast, so that all might remember the holy night of Jesus' birth.

Many such legends tell of how Jesus, Mary, and Joseph were saved from danger through the cooperation of animals and plants, as this retelling of another very old tale illustrates.

*Joseph paused and listened for a moment. He wasn't com*pletely sure, so he ran back a few paces and threw himself down on the ground. With his ear pressed to the dirt, he could feel the vibrations coming through the earth. Cavalry! Herod's soldiers on horseback were pursuing them still.

Joseph was confused and frightened for himself, his wife, and his child. Why were they coming? What was it about his small family that caused the king to react with such violence? What was it that drove him to send out his army with this murderous intent?

It was all beyond Joseph. But then so much of the past few months was beyond him. Dreams and voices, dreams and voices. Telling him that it was all right to wed Mary, that she had not disgraced him. Then last night as he lay in the straw of the stable, trying to make sense of the shepherds' stories about angels singing of the birth of his Jesus as the Messiah, he heard another voice. It was urgent, worried, compelling in its intensity, warning him to flee, to take his family to Egypt, where they would be safe from Herod.

"How could an angel worry?" he wondered as he packed their meagre belongings. Egypt had not been on their itinerary, just a quick trip to Bethlehem to register for the Roman tax and then back to Nazareth. But now it was on to Egypt. He wondered by what providence he had brought his tools. He was a good carpenter; they would not starve in that strange land.

But now in the distance he could hear the hoof beats growing closer. He must move his family quickly if they were to avoid capture.

Desperately, he looked for shelter. There was a small forest of pine trees beside him. In another season, they would drop their needles, but not today: today those needles might just save them. He urged the donkey forward and off the road. They reached the trees just in time and, in the gathering dusk, watched the troops thunder past them down the road. Joseph knew that they would be back, that he could not take that route again.

As the darkness grew, Mary and Joseph and the child moved deeper into the woods. It was growing colder, and they could not risk being caught out in the open. At the centre of the woods stood an ancient pine, gnarled and twisted with age. It was massive, its branches towering high into the night sky. They drew closer and saw that the base of its trunk had been hollowed out. It would be tight, but they all could find shelter there for the night.

The inside of the trunk was warm and dry, fragrant with the scent of pine. Mary and the baby, wrapped in shawl and blanket, fell asleep beside the donkey, warmed by his body. Joseph struggled to stay awake, afraid they might be caught, but as the night stretched on he, too, drifted into desperately needed sleep.

Dawn broke, and with it came the sound of birdsong and the harsh voices of weary soldiers ordered to fulfil a mission they no longer believed in. Joseph sat up, cursing himself for his carelessness. The soldiers were close; they could not run from them. As Mary and the baby slept on, the donkey looked up anxiously, hearing the whinnying of horses. The soldiers were approaching. The sun was rising above the trees, and Joseph knew there was nothing to hide them if a soldier looked into their tree.

As the sun hit the ground and full light travelled to their hiding place, Joseph gasped. Instead of an open passageway, the tree's entrance was a maze of silken webs. In the night, spiders had woven a screen that was now covered in dew. It shimmered in the morning light.

An officer in full armour, sword in hand, passed by the tree, glanced at the opening, and noticed the spiders' work. He raised his sword as if to sweep away that thin barrier, then paused and looked intently at the tree.

"No one's been here but the spiders," he called out. "The child has slipped through our net." Then he stopped for an instant and looked back at the tree. Was Joseph wrong, or did he see the ghost of a smile on the man's lips? "Mount up, back to Jerusalem. They must have gone another way," the soldier said to his mates.

A minute later the soldiers were just a memory. The only sounds were the birds and the creaking of the trees in the light wind.

In later years, Joseph and Mary would talk of that night, of the gift of the tree and the spiders, and wonder about the soldier with the sad, tired eyes who saw but chose not to see. After that night, pine trees never again shed their needles, becoming ever green to mark the night they saved the child of God. The spiders' gift has also been remembered: every piece of shiny tinsel that glitters in the lights on our Christmas trees pays homage to the webs that sparkled in the morning sun and hid Jesus, Joseph, and Mary from Herod's wrath.

But I have told enough stories for now, because I have a critical task that must be completed immediately. Wendy wants my Christmas list. Hmm, what do I want for a gift this year?

On the Sixth Day before Christmas,

my true loves hid from me

six gift items that I kind of,

sort of, hope they might put under

the enormous pine tree.

I like Christmas presents. As I write this, I feel a secret shame. I'm a minister. I'm supposed to be above shameless materialism. I'm supposed to have a holier sense of Christmas. But the sixth day before Christmas finds me loitering in a casual but deliberate manner in front of the Christmas tree. For the packages have started to arrive. Couriers and mail carriers are leaving mysterious cartons inside the screen door. Boxes of intriguing shapes and sizes, wrapped and beribboned, some with my name on them, await my ministrations beneath the pine branches. I try to guess their contents. In the past, I have been known to shake a parcel or two in a vain attempt to unlock their secrets. But my family chases me away from the tree before I succeed.

They know me. They know that Christmas brings out the crazed ten-year-old that lurks within. Forget about my inner child; it's the outer child I become at Christmastime that concerns my nearest and dearest. They know that six days hence I will tear through those boxes, sending wrapping paper flying through the air like confetti at a wedding.

However, the stresses of Christmastime can blunt the keen anticipation of young and old alike.

A few years ago, on the way to ballet class, a

seven-year-old voice from the back of the car uttered these famous words: "Bah, humbug!"

It is not like my Elizabeth to sound like that well-known Dickens character, so I asked what was bothering her.

"It's all this rushing around at Christmas. It makes me feel like Ebenezer Scrooge."

At seven? I can understand that at thirty-seven or forty-seven, but at seven?

Her sister, Sarah, seconded her opinion. "There's too much to do."

So, on the following Saturday, I made an executive decision. I called a halt. We were going to skip skating and ballet lessons. We were going to spend the bulk of the day together as a family. This day the priority was decorating the tree and baking our famous Christmas cookies from my grandmother's recipe. We were going to shop, but for others, not for ourselves.

Each year our church puts together Christmas hampers for those in need. The ages of the children are given out, so we always find a family whose children are the same ages and genders as ours. The rule is that you buy items that your own children would want.

We headed over to the mall, and instead of feeling tired and overwhelmed we were energized and excited. We went through the stores, the girls shopping carefully, looking for toys and clothes that they themselves would like to see under the tree on

Christmas morning. They were exacting in their standards, determined that those two other little girls were going to feel joy on December 25. Our cart filling bit by bit, we moved from store to store until finally everything was found.

When we got home, my little Scrooge looked at the goods laid out on the couch and jumped up and down at the prospect of that other seven-year-old receiving the gifts. Her face was transformed with joy as she looked at me and said, "Daddy, this is really Christmas for me."

Bah, humbug, indeed.

A true gift is a reflection both of the person who gives it and of the person who receives it. When I think back over the course of my life, it is not the gifts themselves I was given that mattered so much as the effort and thought that went into choosing them.

This was especially true when I was a child and even more when I was a teenager. My most memorable family gift came from my parents when I was in grade nine. I was fourteen years old, and it was during my father's Wagner phase. If you are unfamiliar with the works of Richard Wagner, be grateful. He is the heavy metal of the classical music set, and his operas make for grim listening. Each Wagner opera lasts approximately two and a half days. Those days are filled with dragons named

Fafner, giants named Fasolt, and various Valkyries that give the whole art form a bad name. In my teens, the music of Wagner was my constant companion. Morning, noon, and night, out rolled *The Ring of the Nibelung*, and thump, thump, thump went the giants. In our house, it was the children, not the parents, who complained about the volume. We constantly had to tell our parents that, if the sound wasn't turned down, permanent damage would be done to their hearing.

But that Christmas I wanted my own music. Anything non-Wagnerian would do. Specifically, what I dreamed of was *Thick as a Brick* by Jethro Tull, *Tommy* by The Who, and anything by Emerson, Lake and Palmer. I believed these three groups could give old Richard a run for his money.

I was not hopeful. While I knew that Pop could make his way into Sam's or A&A's in downtown Toronto and find the rarest of classical recordings, I was not confident in his ability when faced with racks of rock 'n' roll. Also, there was the memory of the previous year's gift disaster. A chemistry set was on the top of my list that year. I hinted, I was subtle and cunning, and when I saw a large chemistry-set-sized object being hidden at the top of the cupboard in the front hall (a central gift depository), I was confident that soon I would be conducting experiments in my basement that would put Dr. Jekyll to shame.

Imagine my delight when I opened that parcel on Christmas morning to discover not a chemistry set but a large book on flora and fauna. My parents were sure I'd love a biology book because of my fondness for the writings of the British naturalist Gerald Durrell. I kept a smile frozen to my face for hours.

It was, therefore, with a feeling of trepidation and the sense of embracing a lost cause that I handed over my list of wished-for records. My father looked at them in disbelief. How could a child exposed to Wagner, Bach, and Beethoven aspire to own such music? But I was resolute, if not overly hopeful.

The fateful Christmas morning arrived, and we all rushed down and tore into our stockings. When we had devoured the mandarin oranges and admired our new socks and paperback books, we trooped into the dining room for our breakfast, an event that seemed to last longer with each passing year.

Finally, we headed into the living room and distributed the gifts. Parcel after parcel was opened before my dad casually passed me a package that on the surface could be considered the size, shape, and weight of a vinyl LP. As I ripped open the paper, a horrifying thought flashed through my mind: I was about to get my own opera record.

Instead, there they were: Emerson, Lake and Palmer, The Who, and Jethro Tull.

There are many ways a parent can demonstrate

the Christmas spirit to children, but what happened next confirmed Pop's for me. He sent me over to the stereo with my bright, shiny records and told me to play any one I wanted. So that Christmas, instead of "Hark! the Herald Angels Sing" or Handel's *Messiah* we were treated to the seasonal sounds of The Who's "Pinball Wizard'" and ELP's "Lucky Man." (Yes, I managed to sneak in a second record.)

I still have those records. They sit upstairs, part of a long row of vinyl resting below the CDs and tapes. Every now and again I put them on, and through the scratches and the decades-old music I hear an undertone of Christmas and my father's love.

When Wendy and the girls asked me for my Christmas list this year, I thought long and hard.

How about an automatic bread maker? My friends have them, and all swear by the convenience and the joy of waking up to freshly baked bread. Yes, that's what I need, fresh bread. But the more I thought about it, the less appealing it became. When we do make bread in our house, it's a family affair with Sarah and Elizabeth up to their elbows in flour and both of them pounding the life out of the dough. We would lose something by tossing the works into a machine. So forget that idea.

What about a snow blower? Now there's a lot to be said for a snow blower. We have a corner lot, and

I never have enough time to dig out the miles of sidewalk that surround our home. But with a snow blower I could dash through the whole operation in thirty minutes or less and then go back into my nice, snug house.

But, then, practically the only time I actually get to see my neighbours in the winter is when I'm shovelling. Most days the automatic openers pop the garage doors open, and the cars disappear with their occupants. Why, there was one neighbour I didn't see for six months last year. How could we visit with one of those noisy contraptions throwing the snow around? How could I complain about the weather to Gord and Theresa across the street, or Mark and Julie a few houses down, when they're out shovelling their driveways if I'm not?

I could upgrade the speed in my computer, add more RAM or ROM, or whatever it is. What about books? They can be very practical for a minister. Some fancy new aftershave I would never buy myself? But I have a beard.

What to do? What to do? And then it hits me. I know exactly what I want, without doubt, question, or hesitation. What I want for Christmas more than anything else in the world is a tabletop hockey game. That's right, the kind with the plastic nets, the twirly knobs, and the little plastic puck that goes flying over the boards. Not a computer simulation. I want the real thing, the kind where the puck always gets stuck in the net and the playing surface rolls just enough that there are places where the players can't get to the puck.

I had a game like this years ago. I spent hours with it. Whole afternoons would disappear as the Leafs and Canadiens battled for Stanley Cup supremacy. The crowd painted on the boards would roar their approval as the puck rolled down the face-off circle and the game began. Each small metal player had the same hair, face, and teeth, but it didn't matter — in my heart, they were Davey Keon or Jean Beliveau.

Yes, that's it. Table hockey. I'm sure the girls would love playing it with me. And I could call up David and Marc and Larry, and they could come over, and we could spend the afternoon playing, followed by hot chocolate and cinnamon toast.

So, Wendy, there you have it. It doesn't have to be the best 3D model with the realistic faces. It doesn't even have to be new: a garage sale reject will do just fine. But for Christmas, do you think that you and Santa could get together on this one little item? After all, if this is a midlife crisis, it's pretty tame. I could be asking for a Harley!

Gifts, as we all know from personal experience, can be a minefield, especially when it comes to gifts we give to our nearest and dearest.

Last year, with fear and trembling, I broke the cardinal rule in my marriage: I surprised Wendy with a Christmas gift. Completely of my own volition, without the aid of a list or specific instructions as to size, shape, colour, and brand, I risked one whole Christmas. I gambled that, on Christmas morning, my wife would not open the gift with the deadly words "How nice" and the smile that says, "I love him, but he blew it."

Now I am sure there are men out there who are genetically capable of purchasing, without help or guidance, that absolutely perfect gift for their beloved significant others. I, alas, am not among them.

I have tried; honestly, I have. But the infamous dressing gown fiasco early in our marriage scarred me for years. She wanted a dressing gown that year, so I selected with due care what I considered to be an elegant little pink number that tied at the front. It was wrapped and lovingly put under the tree. On that fateful Christmas Day, I eagerly presented the box and awaited the accolades.

Wendy opened the box, lifted out the dressing gown, and uttered one word: "Oh." She disliked pink, wanted comfortable, not elegant, and was hoping for something warm and cozy that would not tie at the front. The day after Boxing Day found me, bruised ego and all, fighting the crowds at the return desk. After that day, I shopped with a detailed list and refused all hints. Unless it was in writing, I was not interested.

Until last year.

My secretary, Sandra, our now retired organist, Ron, and I were sharing some Christmas cheer at lunch when Ron made mention of what has become "the gift." What a great idea! Emboldened, encouraged, and confident that for the first time in over a decade I had discovered the secret desire of Wendy's heart, I rushed out and blew the Christmas budget.

Only when it was too late did I question my actions. Then the spectres of Christmases past rose from the ashes to cloud my eyes. I knew she would love it. It was absolutely perfect, just the thing for a talented mezzo-soprano. She was bound to be thrilled. At least I hoped she was, for this year's gift could be neither returned nor exchanged. I could have been doomed, but no . . . this year would be different. This year would mark the beginning of a whole new trend. Or else I would be looking for company at the Jessye Norman concert this spring. Yes, that was the gift: tickets to hear one of the world's greatest singers.

I am happy to report that, for the first time in our lives, I succeeded not only in surprising my wife but also in delighting her. But I'm still sticking to lists from now on. One successful surprise in a lifetime is probably the maximum allowed to me.

There is no question that deep down we all hope to receive something very special.

My father's most treasured memory was quite different. His goes back to the 1930s, during the Great Depression.

None of us today can appreciate what that generation went through. In western Canada, nature was as depressed as the economy. Severe drought caused the dust bowl, where dirt blew in huge clouds not just for days or months but also for years. Crops failed. In some cases, they couldn't even be planted due to the lack of moisture. Families found themselves in desperate situations. Churches shipped trainloads of food and clothes out west for families that had neither. Farm foreclosures were common. There was no work and no effective government help.

My grandfather was a teacher, and Nana taught piano and gave singing lessons. The family, with four boys, struggled just to get by.

They lived in the then small town of Cochrane, just west of Calgary. Difficult though life was, there were still moments of joy for a small boy. Dad found two great horned owl chicks whose mother had either died or abandoned them. He took them home and raised them on the gophers he would hunt every day. The owls became his constant companions.

The winters in southern Alberta were bitter, and

to help out the family my father ran a trapline in the bush near the Bow River, outside town. He and his dog Laddie would tromp through the snow in minus-forty-degree-Celsius weather, my father's feet covered only in shoes and rubber galoshes. Oh, how he yearned for proper boots: boots lined not with newspaper but with felt or fur. To have warm feet, not feet red and sore from cold and ice, was his chief desire. But my father knew the tenor of the times and said nothing.

Christmas in the Depression was focused on family, if not on presents. It was also a time when parents made great sacrifices for their children. A.E., my grandfather, had four boys to feed. At Christmas dinner, he would declare that he considered the tail portion and neck of their small turkey to be the most delicious and sought after of seasonal delicacies, making a great fuss over the wonders of his choice as his sons devoured drumsticks and breast meat.

When my father woke up on that most memorable Christmas morning, the frost was thick on the windows, and the air was so cold the room filled with fog when he breathed. As he huddled beneath the blankets, he peered over the edge of the bed and saw a parcel, carefully wrapped, on the floor. Not daring to believe it could be possible, he opened the parcel slowly. There, nestled in tissue paper, rested the boots of his dreams. Tall, warm, lined with felt, boots that would keep out the cutting cold and wet. The sacrifices made to pay for them must have been significant.

A few years ago I experienced an autumn at work that gave new meaning to the word *dreadful*. Our church was having what we call a stewardship program, an ecclesiastical version of a PBS pledge drive. Money and the church are sometimes not the happiest of combinations, and the personal toll on me was heavy. The financial results were wonderful, but the process left me limp, ragged, and prone to screaming whenever the phone rang.

In the midst of this, in late October, Wendy and I went Christmas shopping for my sister. A local artist was featuring a collection of hand-carved wooden loons. We wished to purchase one for Alison to open on Christmas morning, when she would be home on her annual pilgrimage from England. We chose the loon. While Wendy was paying for it, I wandered around the gallery looking at the pictures.

It wasn't a particularly remarkable gallery. It was small, the type you would find in shopping malls located anywhere in North America. Then I saw it. A winter scene called *Quiet Morning*. It captured my heart and soul immediately, something that no painting had ever done before.

On the surface, it wasn't a particularly remarkable

picture: a back alley covered in newly fallen snow, a bicycle by a shed on the left, white clapboard, red brick, and brown wooden houses stretching down the alleyway on the right. There are tire ruts in the alley, but they are mostly filled by the yet unbroken snow. The day is just beginning, and nobody is awake. I could actually hear the muffled quiet, that quality of silence that is peculiar to a morning after a heavy snow.

The painting transported me to my own childhood, to the back alleys and byways of north Toronto. I was flooded with memories of toboggans, snow angels, and snow forts.

Wendy came over to see what had caught my attention. I looked at her and then glanced down at the price tag. It was a limited edition print, and the artist was well known enough that the price was far beyond my means. I cast a regretful look back at the painting as we left the store.

Over the next few weeks, I wound up at the mall on numerous occasions. I would always stop to make sure that what I now considered my picture was still there. I would go in, look at it, and feel a sense of badly needed peace and quiet.

Christmas arrived with its usual unseemly haste, and Alison came from England for her visit. Out shopping for the girls, I took her to the gallery. The owner was getting used to seeing me by now, and smiled as I walked in. I took my bemused sister to the wall where my painting was hanging . . . but it was gone.

You know how Tiny Tim's face falls in the old black-and-white version of *A Christmas Carol* when his favourite toy is removed from the store window? That was me. Dolefully, I finished the shopping and went home and reported its loss to my wife.

Christmas morning dawned, and we crawled downstairs in the dark to join our excited and eager daughters. We opened our gifts and oohed and aahed over the various parcels as the sun came up. I was busy trying to figure out the latest fiendish puzzle that my sister had stuffed into my stocking when Wendy came up bearing a large, flat, rectangular parcel.

I tore it open with my usual sense of dignity. It was the painting! I felt a sense of true wonder. "You couldn't have," I started to say. "We can't afford —"

Wendy cut me off. "You always make sure everyone else is looked after at Christmas, that we all have nice things, so this is your year," she said.

"But how . . ." I spluttered.

"Simple," she said. "I put aside all the money I made from leading the Durham choir, from teaching, and from singing the solos in the *Messiah*."

Wendy and I have been together since we were nineteen years old. We've been married for two decades. I looked at her and felt like I was seeing her again for the first time. It was one of those magic moments in a marriage when one partner acts out of total love for the other. And it was the utter unselfishness of the act that transformed that print into something better than a Leonardo da Vinci original.

The picture now hangs above the couch in the living room. You see it as soon as you walk in the door. When I feel tired and frazzled, I sit and let that early morning winter scene wash over me. It always gives me a great sense of peace.

On the Fifth Day before Christmas,

the call went out from me

for five Thespian goats

(and please keep them away

from the enormous pine tree).

This time of year never goes by without reminiscences about the greatest pre-Christmas disaster I ever faced. It was five days before Christmas, and I had no goats for our Christmas Eve production.

Goats? Why on Earth would I need goats for the 24th of December?

It's simple, really. Each Christmas Eve for the past decade, the young people of Westminster United have put on a play or a musical at our two family services, a production complete with costumes, lights, and, of course, the real stars of the show, the animals.

Jesus, as we know, was born in a stable. So what could be more authentic than celebrating his birth with sheep, goats, ducks, and other representatives of the animal kingdom?

I wish I could take full credit for this act of inspired genius, but, alas, I cannot. I must tip my hat to a white clapboard country church in the Alberta community of Springbank. For it was there, in my very first church, that it all began. The youth group and their leader, Wally, approached me with the idea of creating a play for Christmas Eve. I happily agreed, and then, as if it was an idea that had just, at that moment, come to them, they quietly added, "Oh, and we thought we'd have a couple of animals."

"How fitting," I thought to myself, "some cats, a puppy, and a pet rabbit, what can it hurt?" I should have noticed the gleams in their eyes. On the day before Christmas, late in the afternoon, I was changing into my gown when what sounded like a stampede erupted outside my office. Hooves! I actually heard the sounds of hooves! I yanked open my door, and there in front of my disbelieving eyes were a goat, a sheep, two ducks, and a dog. The goat and the sheep proceeded to wish me the best of the season by urinating copiously and in tandem at my feet, much to the amusement of the assembled cast. "Ah, well," I thought to myself, "better here than in the church." But I underestimated that sheep.

The play had gone well, the animals had behaved magnificently, and, just when I thought we were going to emerge unscathed, the sheep uttered a loud baa, lifted his tail, and disgraced himself with unerring accuracy on the one part of the sanctuary carpet that was not covered in plastic. It gave us that final touch of stablelike authenticity, an authenticity the assembled congregation had probably not anticipated when they had set out for church that night.

But a tradition was born that evening, one I brought with me to Whitby. When I first arrived at Westminster and made this suggestion regarding the youth and the animals, the church board looked at me as though I was unhinged. This church was surrounded not by farmers' fields but by subdivisions. Where would we even get the animals? But I persevered and found a genuine sheep farm just north of town. And so we launched our first annual Christmas Eve with creatures. It was a huge success and now draws people from all over the region.

Animals do add interesting wrinkles to Christmas Eve productions.

Take the duck incident two years ago. Our sheep supplier had tossed in a few ducks so that the avian world would be represented at the birth. We were unaware at the time that ducks could bite. In fact, while one was happy and content, the other nibbled on his handler repeatedly. Fortunately, the handler was a doctor and could heal himself of any damage that resulted from being beaked. We assumed, incorrectly, that the ducks' wings were clipped. Only a last-minute tackle prevented one duck from becoming airborne and migrating into the congregation for the winter. There are many images of Christmas that a minister hopes his own flock will retain. Their minister chasing a flying duck through the church is not among them. The ducks were retired to private life.

Then there were the sheep. There is the saying "as stubborn as a mule." Forget it. It should be "as stubborn as a sheep." We have had sheep that have stopped halfway down the aisle and said, "That's close enough." Or sheep that have been so moved by the church experience that they would not leave the front — convinced, no doubt, that the man dressed in the white gown was some form of close relative with whom they had a deep and abiding desire to flock. Forget the movie *Babe*. I could have baaed all night, and they still wouldn't have moved.

Going back a ways, there was Springbank's year of the pig. Biblically and geographically, the chances of a Vietnamese pot-bellied pig being anywhere near a stable in Palestine two thousand years ago were simply nil. However, much to my surprise, Charlotte appeared one Christmas Eve. Her owner assured me that what we lacked in scriptural accuracy would be more than compensated for in charm and panache. "Vietnamese pot-bellied pigs," she said with fervour, "make wonderful pets and will get along with all our other cast members, both those on four and those on two legs."

As my cast beseeched me to include Charlotte, I caved in. Never had I made such an error, and divine retribution was on its way.

Pot-bellied pigs have the reputation of being sociable and engaging but not especially loud creatures. Charlotte, at first glance, appeared thrilled to be among us. As the play got under way, she snuffled, she grunted, she made, from what I could tell, happy pig noises. But then she spotted the sheep. I do not know what trauma she had experienced among sheep in the past, but apparently it must have been significant. Once she saw them, Charlotte protested her involvement in the whole affair.

Vietnamese pigs, I learned that night, have vocal abilities that far outweigh the volumes produced by an organ, a choir, and a congregation, all producing decibels at full throttle. We were overwhelmed by this one innocuous-seeming pig. The sanctuary echoed with pot-bellied protests so loud you would have sworn that banks of speakers had been installed just for her. Apparently, pigs don't need to breathe, because Charlotte never stopped or even paused. I was drowned out, my cast was drowned out. The noise irritated the dogs, which started to bark, and this set off the sheep, which baaed, stamped their feet, and looked as though they were getting ready to stampede through the church.

I gestured urgently to Charlotte's chagrined owner to remove the pig. Charlotte, however, was having none of this. Having arrived at church, she was determined to remain there. It took a team of ushers to remove her from the premises and back to her trailer. The service continued, but it just wasn't the same somehow. We could still hear her through the walls.

But back to that one year's goat crisis. Weeks and weeks of rehearsals were behind us, hundreds and hundreds of people had circled the date on their calendars, and nary a goat was in sight. What to do, what to do?

I wrote a plea for help in my newspaper column, but that was not enough, for this was an emergency not just of local, but also of national, significance. There was only one option. For a number of years, I was a regular contributor to the CBC national radio program *Morningside*. I faxed a letter to its famous host, Peter Gzowski, requesting his assistance.

"Peter," I wrote. "I need goats. Not a lot, not a flock, or a herd, or a gaggle, just a couple for church. That's right, church. But not for this Sunday. No, this is for a special command performance at 5:00 p.m. and 7:00 p.m. this coming Christmas Eve."

I went on to tell Peter that part of our Westminster tradition was to have our youth put on a Christmas play at our two early services. The dénouement, the highlight, the pièce de résistance is the arrival of the animals coming down the aisle to re-create the visit of the shepherds to the stable in Bethlehem. Animals provide that element of unpredictability that adds so much to Christmas Eve, I explained to him.

Why goats, you ask again? Because the year before we had entered nirvana courtesy of goats. Our sheep supplier, after many years of faithful service, had retired, sold the farm, and gone into television commercials, extolling a brand of chocolate Easter eggs. Where, I wondered, would we get the animals?

But I failed to take into account a well-known member of our congregation who works in the parks and recreation department. He had goat connections. That's right. He knew of two goats that might be available for that night. They were delivered on time, and what a performance they gave! They were positively regal — and housebroken to boot!

Down the aisle they went, acknowledging the cheering throng, bobbing their heads from time to time in a rather dignified manner, and then graciously making their exit on cue. I was ready to sign them up for a lifetime contract on the spot and move them into my garage if necessary. They could trim the grass in summer, whatever they wanted. But, sadly, the competition was too fierce, and the goats were sold to another buyer. (I suspect the Presbyterians.)

I was ecstatic when Gzowski agreed to read my entreaty on the air.

> Does anyone out there have a few goats that have always yearned to expand their horizons and come to church on Christmas Eve? Goats that have wanted to leave the field for the bright lights? Call, fax, e-mail me. My lines are open. Auditions are not necessary. It's a walk-on part.

After Gzowski and cohost Shelagh Rogers had finished reading my cross-Canada plea that Friday at 10:30 a.m., Gzowski phoned me. "Good luck, Chris," he said, stifling laughter.

At precisely 10:32 a.m., the phone rang. "Good morning, Christopher White speaking," I said eagerly.

The person on the other end sounded breathless. "I just listened to the radio and heard your request. I knew I had to call you. I have twelve goats, all gentle and easy to work with."

Twelve goats! A miracle! My mind started racing. Where to put them all? Goats at the front door, goats in the lobby, goats on the balcony, goats everywhere. A real, honest-to-goodness Christmas flock. That should top the Baptist Church's camel of last year. I even started to wonder if we could arrange for that elephant from the Bowmanville Zoo to drop by.

My benefactor continued, "Yes, they're very gentle. I raised my children with them. We make soap from the milk. It's really quite wonderful."

Delighted though I was to learn of the goats' belief in cleanliness being next to godliness, I was impatient and wanted to close the deal. "Do you have a trailer? Can you deliver them, or do you need us to pick them up?" I asked.

There was a long pause on the line. "Well, this may pose a small problem. We don't have a trailer."

Quickly, I considered my alternatives. "If we can

get a trailer, can we have them?"

"Oh, yes, they are here if you want them."

"Terrific," said I. "By the way, where exactly is 'here'?"

Another long pause. "It's a little bit of a drive," she confessed sheepishly.

"How little?" I inquired.

"Not too far. I live just outside of Ottawa, so it's only four hours."

With that, my precious goats disappeared into thin air faster than S. Claus going up the chimney.

The phone kept ringing. A gentleman offered to be my goat broker and scour Durham region from one end to the other. Offers of bunnies, cats, and dogs poured in. A member of my congregation kindly volunteered the use of her new ferret. I checked the Bible. No ferrets. I was also concerned that the ferret might try to eat the rabbits, which would not convey the image of peace and goodwill toward all I was hoping for.

Every path was a blind alley. Despite all those people trying for us, coast to coast, I had no goats. With the days racing toward Christmas, I called Debbie, our goat lady of the previous year. I begged, I cajoled. Could she possibly track down the new owners of those goats and intercede for us? Debbie could make no promises. But she and prayer were all we had.

I waited anxiously, jumping whenever the phone rang, but still no word. I was starting to wonder whom in my church I could convince to dress up as a goat.

Then, twenty-four hours before the performance, Debbie called. Good news, wonderful news, we had goats. Last year's stars were prepared for an encore performance. Between the goats, the bunnies, a couple of kittens, and a real sheepdog, we would be just fine. Thank you, Debbie.

Since then we have relied on the Oshawa Zoo for all our goat needs. Its well-bred goats are trained for walk-on leads! Heaven for the shepherds. But as for the housebreaking aspect of their training, they are not at one hundred percent. I had to apologize profoundly to one woman as she put on her boots following the 5:00 p.m. service last year. There are some things one truly does not wish to find in a stocking.

Every Christmas production has its own unique flavour, depending on the subject of the play to be performed.

While most people spend August sitting outside, slathering on sunscreen by the barbecue, I am closeted in my office, surrounded by stacks of books, desperately searching for just the right story to adapt. We have performed *A Christmas Carol*, our own *It's a Whitby Wonderful Life*, featuring not an angel named Charlie but Charlie's Angels. And one year we put on an original musical written by our organist, Margaret.

But my favourite of all was a Yuletide version of *Les Miserables* that I found in a dusty old book of Christmas plays. *Les Miz* is close to my heart, not just because of the story, which is wonderful, but also because of the circumstances surrounding the four times I have seen it.

The last time was with Sarah. Wendy had gone into Toronto for her staff lunch. As part of Sarah's Christmas gift, she had purchased two rush seats to that afternoon's performance of *Les Miserables*. For twenty dollars each, it was the best deal in theatre. So I pulled Sarah out of school for the afternoon and, for the fourth time in my life, went to see my all-time favourite musical.

Our seats were up in the top balcony and along the side rail, so we had to lean a little to see the full stage, but otherwise the sight lines were great and the sound superb. Sarah was convinced that they were the best seats in the house, and when, at intermission, I suggested trying to snag a couple of empty seats in the orchestra she refused. She loved looking down at the audience and felt the plush chairs we were sitting on were the height of elegance.

As for the musical, it was, in the words of my then almost-eleven-year-old daughter, "the most awesome, spectacular thing I have ever seen." All I can say is "Ditto."

Each time I have watched that musical, it has affected me in different ways. The first time Sarah was just over a year old and had been hospitalized twice in Calgary with severe asthma. We were visiting Toronto for the summer holidays, and Wendy and I were given tickets by her parents. When little Cosette came onstage carrying her bucket, singing "Castle in the Clouds," we both burst into tears.

The next summer we went again, with my parents. This time I was fine until Jean Valjean's signature song, "Bring Him Home." My mom was sitting beside me, and when Michael Burgess started singing she reached for my hand and held onto it for dear life. I knew she was remembering the day I'd left for West Africa. I had never before seen my mom genuinely afraid, not in the twenty-five years she had been battling cancer. But that day at the airport when I left them, I saw the fear in her eyes. She was afraid that something would happen to me overseas. Almost five months later — and twenty-five pounds lighter due to the effects of malaria — I returned. When I got off the plane, my mom almost cracked my ribs, she hugged me so hard. Now, as "Bring Him Home" drew to its conclusion, she started to cry, and I started to snuffle.

The next year we were supposed to go with friends of ours to the road show version of *Les Miz*, which had landed in Calgary. Instead, we were back in Toronto, attending my mother's funeral. The cancer had finally won.

That was it, until six years later, when *Les Miz* returned to Toronto. By that time, we were living in southern Ontario, and for the third time we headed to the theatre. I was sure I wouldn't need Kleenex this time. But then Colm Wilkinson started singing "Bring Him Home." This time it was Wendy holding my hand, and I knew she was remembering everything we had been through together. By now our younger daughter had been born with cardiac complications and had gone through three heart surgeries. Wendy started crying, and again I wasn't far behind.

By the time Sarah and I got to the show, I was absolutely confident: no tears this fourth time. But darn that Colm Wilkinson! He sang so powerfully that Sarah started sobbing her heart out, holding onto me with both hands. Obviously, the rarefied air in the balcony was affecting my eyes, because they started watering like crazy.

That Christmas Eve, we performed the Christmas-play version of *Les Miz*, which I had adapted for our church youth group (Victor Hugo didn't include the nativity story and live goats). We had been rehearsing for weeks, and not one tear had I shed. That night, when the kids performed at the two services, I didn't cry, even though it was the last year for cast members Ken, Marissa, Robyn, and Janya as they were about to head off to university. No, I didn't cry, not even when we gave them their stuffed sheep, a tradition for all graduating cast members.

I never shed a single tear . . . until the drive home.

The play and the animals are only part of the equation. There is also the cast. Each production I have been involved with has its own rhythm.

Sometime in October, having examined every Christmas play known to humankind, I announce auditions. On a Sunday, after worship and following coffee time, which is the busiest thirty minutes of my week, I head back into the sanctuary. There, sprawled at the front or lounging among the pews, are fifteen to twenty teenagers, munching sandwiches or fries, drinking pop, and talking to each other a mile a minute. The veterans are quite cool, but the kids who are here for their first year look nervous. This is a significant rite of passage in our church. The youth of our congregation grow up waiting impatiently until they are old enough to be part of it. Those who have graduated into postsecondary education and jobs look back on these productions as the highlights of their church lives.

Our production team consists of me as writer, adapter, director, and producer; Margaret, our organist, as musical director; and Marissa, back from university, Shiona on makeup, Duncan lights and sound, Lisa on choreography and a couple of parent volunteers. The scripts are distributed, but they are not yet finished. The reason for this is simple enough. I keep adding parts and lines over the next couple of weeks as my cast grows.

The first candidate mounts the small platform at the front of the sanctuary and reads a part. Not bad: good voice, comfortable presence on stage.

"Thank you. Next," I call out.

For about an hour, a constant flow of teenagers read various lines and parts. Some are great; some . . . have potential greatness.

Over the next week, we meet and attempt to assign roles. This is tricky. Seniority counts in our production; the closer you are to graduation, the better your chance for a significant part. First-year players get lines, though, and every now and then one talent so impresses it cannot be ignored. Phone calls are made, parts are assigned, general happiness reigns. Depending on the year and the play, we usually double-cast the leads, one for each service. We want everyone to have a good experience. The adage "There are no small parts" is said more than once.

The following week we begin in earnest. Practice schedules are distributed; the date for the dress rehearsal is announced. I stress again and again and again the date by which all parts must be memorized.

A play is produced by layers. First, the actors read the scripts through. When they are comfortable with the parts, we start adding staging, the music, the choreography, and finally the costumes and props.

During the early practices, laughter and jokes dominate the stage as my cast gets familiar with both the material and each other. I can be found in various parts of the sanctuary, watching from all vantage points, occasionally shouting out instructions and constantly calling for silence.

When you work year after year with teenagers, you quickly learn a few things. First, you will never, no matter how many times you beg, plead, and threaten, ever have your full cast present until the actual performance. Second, 99.9% of all casts require "the speech." The speech is delivered when you have rehearsed for weeks and are in genuine terror of sharing what they have produced with the general public. This bit of rhetoric must be carefully crafted and exquisitely timed, neither too angry nor too dramatic. It must adopt a mournful tone that implies regret over the fact that instead of a play the congregation is going to get an hour-long Christmas carol sing if things don't shape up. A tone that suggests they can rise above this current level of despair and offer something inspired and hope-filled. A reminder that I could be home watching the football game never goes amiss. But never ever bluff; mean what you say, or you are doomed, for they can sense your fear. This speech in my experience actually works, but, and this is key, you can deliver it only once each season. It's another Christmas tradition, a sign that it's time to get to work because Christopher has started foaming at the mouth . . . again.

With lines mostly memorized, we proceed with the staging. Due to the unique shape of our sanctuary, sight lines from the side are not great. So I am constantly shouting, "Front, front, you have to stand right near the front, remember the poor schleb in the back corner."

The worst seat in the house lies in the southeast corner of our overflow area. It's the end of the back row, and that person's only hope of seeing the play is if the performers stand right near the edge of the platform. "Remember the poor schleb" becomes our rallying cry as we walk through the staging process. I'm thinking of taping a welcome letter to that chair next year, letting that person know how many weeks we have been thinking of him or her and wishing that person a special Christmas welcome. I could inform him or her that for weeks I sat right there as the company rehearsed, producing the whole play with that person in mind. I'll just have to come up with a slightly more decorous and festive term than "poor schleb" — perhaps "gracious patron" or "most blessed congregant." I'll work on it.

As we draw closer to the date, intensity and tension build. I shout more; they listen more. I start praising their performances; they critique themselves. They're much harder on themselves than I ever would be. After each run-through, I ask them what went well and what needs to be improved. We go over it again and again, music, choreography, in with the props, practise, practise, practise. We fuel them with doughnuts, sour cherry blasters, and Fuzzy Peaches.

Then it happens: the annual miracle. Instead of a disparate group of adolescents, I have a cast of actors. Actors who care, actors who are about to create Christmas magic. We can all feel that transitional moment. It happens at a different time each year, but it always happens. The kids are filled with pride in their accomplishment; they believe in themselves as the characters they play.

We draw closer to C Day. Five days left, one dress rehearsal to go. "Places everyone, and please remember the 'special guest' in the back corner."

All is set. Now I have to head over to the next rehearsal. This one is filled with children getting ready for the annual Sunday school pageant.

On the Fourth Day before Christmas,

we practised at the church

with four- and five-year-old shepherds,

who fought under the enormous pine tree.

"Shepherds to the left!" calls out the director. "Wise men — where are my wise men, and who put the angels upstairs?"

Children dressed as sheep, cows, and horses suddenly appear unbidden on the stage, trailing two desperate parent volunteers. Four of the shepherds have decided that their crooks are in fact ninja weapons, and they begin a clash that quickly deteriorates into *Crouching Shepherd, Hidden Sheep*. The teenage narrators gaze upon the chaos with a combination of disdain and nostalgia. Two small figures dressed as Mary and Joseph get into a tug of war over the doll who represents the reason for the whole event, doing damage that just isn't in the spirit of the season.

The junior-choir director attempts to coax sounds from her charges, who have been struck simultaneously with amnesia and muteness. Meanwhile, the biblical scenery of palm trees, desert-style buildings, and landscapes that seemed so sturdy when built turns out not to have the strength to withstand a group of roving eight-year-olds.

"Timber," calls out a father as a palm tree heads straight to the stage floor. The sound system, which has just been rented at not insignificant expense, fills the auditorium with the high-pitched squeal of feedback. Thinking that this is his cue, the stage manager closes the curtain on the assembled cast. Three two-year-old angels burst into tears, and the director feels like joining in.

It's the annual children's Christmas pageant. Goodwill and peace to all. Well, maybe after the dress rehearsal, if we're still talking to each other.

If there is one thing guaranteed to get a minister's blood to run cold, it's the prospect of the annual Sunday school pageant. This event requires that you come up with something traditional yet innovative, unique without being too different. It is the Mount Everest of clerical challenges.

Each October the Sunday school coordinators appear at the church with happy, nay hopeful, faces gazing at you with the most vexing question of the year: "What are we going to do this Christmas?" They are certain you know, confident that hidden up your sleeve, on the tip of your tongue, is a plan so creative, so steeped in both tradition and contemporary reality, that it will allow everybody to rediscover the true meaning of Christmas.

So you nod wisely, tell them that everything is well in hand, you have plans, new ideas brewing, none quite ready to be revealed, but soon all will be made clear. You stand up, head toward the door leading to the safety of your office. Then, pausing briefly, you turn, as if the thought has just now come to you, and say, "If any of you has an idea, I would be more than happy to incorporate it into the pageant. In fact, we could go with whatever you come up with." You flash a pastoral smile, then quickly exit, hoping the phone will ring in the next few days with an idea that will save the day.

But, strangely, the phone remains silent. Days, even weeks, pass, and it refuses to ring. And finally the truth dawns: more meetings must be called, and you are going to have to help come up with something . . . anything. A pageant concept must be created and fleshed out, a production team built. Then let the rehearsals begin.

There are certain unwritten rules that define a Sunday school Christmas pageant. The first of these deals with costumes. All children who are either shepherds or Joseph will be dressed in their bathrobes. Colours that I suspect were not around during biblical times will shine forth from the stage, blinding us with their brightness. I just hope, as I do every year, that Power Rangers, Barney, the latest Disney character, or the face of the captain of the Maple Leafs will not be beaming down at us when the words "And there were shepherds watching over their flock by night" are read aloud.

But it's a faint hope. To match the bathrobes, towels of various hues and shades will be draped over children's heads and with luck might stay on for longer than thirty seconds. The reactions of the children when their towels fall off vary. Some shrug and just stick them back on their heads; others wave them around in an attempt to whip the crowd into a frenzy. There are children, mainly but not always of the male variety, who will use them as offensive weapons, flicking their neighbours.

Occasionally, towel loss is the final straw for a child. He gets through the rehearsals, deals with the pressure, the stage, the flashing cameras, and all those people. Then the child stares at the towel now sitting on the floor. Tears welling and a scream forming, he flees the stage. Such children are announcing in the language of four-year-olds that they cannot be expected to work under these conditions. Parents immediately leap to their feet and run backstage in the vain hope they can coax their youngster back into the spotlights.

If shepherds and wise men come fully equipped with bathrobes, angels are a different matter. Their costumes are invariably made of Dad's, Grandpa's, or Uncle's white shirts. I myself discovered one December Saturday that my closet was lighter by two of my favourite shirts. The shirts are enhanced by the addition of cardboard wings covered in aluminum foil, fastened with safety pins or glue. A small garland on the head forms the perfect halo. Add some glitter, and you are all set.

With angels, it's the wings that can cause problems. Children crowded together can knock them off, or some enterprising souls may decide to see if they can actually fly, launching themselves off the stage and onto the gym mats laid out for the performers to sit on when not onstage.

A Sunday school concert is not for the faint of heart. The biblical Christmas story is the focus of this presentation, so Santa, who is everywhere else in evidence, is excused from attendance. His ancestor, Saint Nicholas, may well make an appearance but only as a featured character replaying the stocking tale. (This well-known story involves Nicholas, then a bishop in Turkey. He learned of a poor family with three daughters, who had no dowry. Without a dowry, they could not be married, so Nicholas secretly dropped gold coins into their stockings when they were hanging out to dry. The girls not only had a dowry, but there was also money left over for the family. Our tradition of hanging stockings by the fireplace evolved from that act of generosity.)

Besides the above-mentioned characters, our cast must include sheep, an innkeeper, the innkeeper's wife, a donkey, and some camels.

Of course, some may want to quibble with details. Some scholars say the Magi — a.k.a. the three wise men — did not arrive with their gold, frankincense, and myrrh at the same time as the shepherds. But so what? The issue is the deep truth of the Christmas story. When small children dressed as shepherds and angels sing "Away in a Manger," people will cry. It can't be helped. No person with a heart can listen to those little ones sing that hymn without getting weepy. There are several possible reasons for this: you have a child onstage; you have a grandchild onstage; you remember when you had a child onstage; you have a vague, just-met-them-for-the-first-time connection to a child onstage; or you remember when *you* were the child onstage. Any of these is more than enough.

It's the power of Christmas. It's the power of the story. Of a child born in a stable, the family alone at night, the bright star shining down, soldiers searching for them. It touches us at our most elemental level, our desire to protect the most vulnerable person on Earth, a newborn baby. It is incarnation in its most intimate form that we experience. That's why these concerts touch us so deeply. Seeing our children playing those parts can pack an emotional wallop.

But sometimes the pageant produces laughter, not tears. For example, two years ago Elizabeth had a key role in narrating the Christmas pageant. The service was held down at the local school, where there would be room for everybody. Lizzy was to come out from behind the curtain on cue and deliver her lines. The moment came; we waited, then waited some more. No Liz. The director ran backstage; meanwhile, out came Liz looking for her cue from the director. The director was not there, so she went back behind the curtain. Naturally, the director had just come back out front. Not seeing Liz, backstage she dashed again. This could have gone on for days, months, years even. Eventually, they connected, and the lines were delivered.

There are a couple of approaches that you can take to a Christmas pageant. You can simply reenact the Christmas story. This always works. It is a tale that remains fresh. You can use a theme such as "Christmas around the world" or "Christmas throughout the ages." But my favourite is to go the interactive route and create a full-fledged Bethlehem market.

A Bethlehem market gives that wonderful combination of tradition and chaos. It's highly participatory since both the cast and the congregation become involved. We held ours in the gym of the school down the street, transforming the space into a village and marketplace. Various booths were set up around the gym's perimeter and draped in wonderful fabrics. One was a kitchen, where the children helped to cook food from recipes dating back to biblical times. Another had basket weavers demonstrating the skills of their trade. We set up a pottery wheel and manned it with children, who made clay pots. We devised a fabric booth, where weaving took place, and a scribe's shop, where the children did calligraphy. Of course, what would a market be without the famous inn, complete with innkeepers explaining how they had no room because of the census? Add to this Roman soldiers demanding bribes from the merchants, arresting the people and tossing them in jail, as well as beggars, pickpockets, and escaped slaves running through the market, and you've got quite an event. The congregation walked through it all, adding to the noise and the chaos. At the end, we all gathered for a more formal worship to celebrate and give thanks.

I love this approach, but since we did it just last year I had to come up with a new idea for this Christmas.

I started by calling my denomination's resource centre and asking it to send me everything that in any shape or form resembled a pageant script. Within days, booklet after booklet poured in. Surely, I thought, one of these will contain the solution.

But they didn't. They were too familiar. If the pageant is too much like last year's, the magic disappears, and people feel as though they are going through the motions.

I checked the library and surfed the Internet, but nothing caught the spirit of the season for me. There was only one solution: I called my friend Bob.

To my congregation, Bob is a man of mystery. I will, from time to time, open my sermon with the sentence "I had lunch with my friend Bob last week" and then tell a story of what happened to us. In the ten years I have been at Westminster, the members of my church have never actually seen my friend Bob. There are three theories making the rounds.

Some say that Bob is my version of Maris, Niles's ex-wife on the television program *Frasier*. She is talked about, everyone knows her, but she is never actually seen. So perhaps Bob is a fictional character I have invented as a sort of sermon equivalent to a literary device.

The second theory is that Bob exists but that I'm the only one who can actually see or talk to him. Bob, in this view, is my version of Harvey, the invisible, six-foot-tall rabbit that kept following Jimmy Stewart around in the old movie of the same name.

The third theory is that Bob is real but can't actually be like the man in the stories I tell.

But he is real, I tell you, and the stories are true! For my congregation and all others, let me confirm in print once and for all that Bob is as real as Santa and Christmas. There, that should answer any and all questions.

Bob is my best friend. We have known each other since seminary, where we would spend some of our finest hours in the lounge drinking coffee and talking. Bob graduated with enough academic awards to start his own college, but instead of pursuing a doctorate he chose to go into pastoral ministry. He was placed in a small outport village in Newfoundland. In my first parish, in Springbank, I gazed on the Rockies and participated in a cattle roundup and branding. Bob, meanwhile, was learning about cod and was gazing across the vast expanse of the Atlantic Ocean.

We corresponded over the years, and when we both returned to Ontario we reconnected. Bob's new church was in the western part of southern Ontario, and mine was in the eastern part.

Bob and I call each other on Monday morning, debrief from Sunday, talk about what went well and what we wish we could do all over again. While every parish is different, every parish is similar, so we feed ideas to each other on how to survive. One of our highlights is a monthly lunch in Toronto.

Our pattern never varies. One of us is usually running late, but we end up together in a booth in a restaurant overlooking Yonge and Eglinton.

We like to watch the streetscape below us as we eat. It is always theatre in the best sense of the word. From our second-floor perspective, we can see everything. The bored limo driver, illegally parked, watching for both the police and his patron. The young lovers who meet by the statues in the plaza. Teenagers from the local high school displaying metalwork attached to various parts of their anatomies. The business people in perpetual motion, cellphones attached to their ears, computers in their palms, their tension emanating up to our seats. The street preacher who excoriates the crowd that the end is near. Young moms with children in strollers. One or two homeless people, sitting still, hands or caps out, selling the street newspaper or hoping for some change and a little eye contact.

This is the neighbourhood where Wendy and I courted. I gave Wendy her engagement ring in front of the library just behind this building. She used to work in the summers at this mall, and I would meet her at the end of her shift. We would go to a movie or for long summer walks, wondering what our future would bring. From my window, I can see the bus station bay where I would catch the last bus home at night. Dad never slept; he always peered at me and his watch simultaneously as I walked in the door.

On this occasion, Bob and I compared church notes and talked about our families and what it's like to be married to a teacher (both of our wives went back to school for their teaching degrees just a few short years ago). We paid our bill and headed over to the bookstore next door. We cruised the aisles, picked up a book or two that looked helpful for our work, and then sat down at the café at the front of the store.

I was filled with anticipation when Bob opened his small satchel, for within it, I was sure, lay the only hope for my Christmas pageant. On this subject, my brain was in dry dock.

"Fear not," said Bob. "Here is a foolproof program."

Before sharing his concept with you, I need to let you know that Bob's congregation consists of townsfolk and farmer folk. So Bob is a font of wisdom on agricultural matters.

Take, for instance, the issue of milking cows. I have, in fact, milked a cow, just once, and was thrilled to see the jet of milk stream into the bucket. I still have a mythological view of farming. If you really push me, I'll admit that the beverage in the bag in my refrigerator did not come from cows with names that were hand-milked for my drinking pleasure. But I had no idea until recently what really happens in contemporary agriculture. In the farm of today, each cow has a computer chip embedded in an ear tag. A cow wishing to be milked has options of which her ancestors could only dream. Our computer-enhanced cow goes up to a gate that, upon scanning her chip, opens. The cow then proceeds to walk up and over a raised platform. At the end of the platform sits a feeding station where high-quality grain is dispensed upon her arrival. As the cow begins to feed, up pops the milking robot from below. The robot washes the udder and then attaches the apparatus, which milks the cow, measuring and recording her output. When the milking is complete, the food stops. Another gate opens, and the cow exits. The cow is allowed only so many trips per day. Because each milking is recorded on the computer, if she exceeds that number the gate will not open.

This is cow.com. Today's farmer is both an animal expert and a computer whiz. I don't think that any of the animals in Jesus' stable were wired, but it certainly opens the door for some interesting possible updates on the story.

But Bob is not a fan of the high-tech world, so his pageant is refreshingly free of computers and electronic devices. His production occurs not in a church or a school auditorium but in a barn. A real, live, 150-year-old Ontario barn. This barn is the height of a three-storey building, and its interior measures sixty by one hundred feet. In this unheated barn, the congregation gathers to watch Bob's production. Since it is December, it is very cold in the barn, but people crowd in, dressed in their warmest winter gear. Some stand; others sit on straw bales. The nativity characters mill around attired in the requisite bathrobes put on top of coats, with towels on their heads, a few toques peeking out from underneath. There is neither organ nor keyboard, not even a guitar. The service opens and closes with everyone singing a cappella. It's so cold you can see their breath carrying mist throughout the barn.

After the first hymn, out bounds Bob. His ensemble is not considered usual in clerical circles: big black rubber boots, white corduroys, white sweater, and a white hat with black ears sewn on. He is a sheep. Words fail me as I try to grasp the concept of my friend Bob as livestock. But it is true nonetheless.

"Baa, baa," he bleats in greeting and then continues:

Welcome to Bethlehem. Welcome to my barn. I hope you find it cozy on a winter's night. Isn't it a strange and wonderful night? Here you are in a chilly barn, when you could be snug and warm at home. And here I am speaking to you, instead of silently munching away on my feed. Strange and wonderful — you'd almost think that something was going to happen here tonight. I suppose you came to register for the tax, just like the rest of them. Did you travel far? Not as far as one family. They came all the way from Nazareth, a very long way indeed. They went into town, but there were so many people come for the tax there was no room for them in the inn. So they came here. We can always make room for a few more in the barn. They are so cold and tired. What is more, the woman is going to have a baby and soon. This is Christmas Eve. A story is going to happen, and you are a part of it. . . .

With that, a very simple service continues. The gospel accounts of Jesus' birth are read. During the readings, children dressed as the familiar characters act out their roles. Then much-loved carols are sung, and at the end of the service Mary and Joseph depart with my baaing buddy. There are calves in pens for the children to see, and even though it is, in Bob's words, "colder than blazes" everyone has a wonderful time. No unintentional acts of violence between cast members; the only tears are from the congregation.

It's a mystical moment. Christmas comes alive; Bethlehem is not a distant land but a current reality.

I am ecstatic: I have in my hands this year's Christmas pageant.

Upon reaching home, I leap into action.

Where can I find a barn, I wonder? A real, live barn, with real, live animals. I call Bob, no, not that Bob, another Bob. He and my colleague Gail live on a farm east of Oshawa. Huge barn, enormous barn, big enough to hold everyone with room for relatives. Tragically, this Bob informs me it is not a working barn, and he couldn't guarantee our safety. Broken limbs, contusions, and lawsuits are to be avoided at all costs. Where to go, where to go?

Then it strikes me. North of Whitby sits Windreach Farms, a working farm designed for and run by the disabled. We have had our church picnic there a number of times. The wonderfully big barn has two floors: an open upstairs with benches for sitting and stables below with donkeys, sheep, goats, and a Vietnamese pot-bellied pig. It's a sign, I tell you, it's a sign!

I call immediately, breathless with anticipation. Peggy, the chief administrator, answers the phone. She is excited — she has always wanted something like this to happen on the farm. We could hold the service in the barn and then have cider in the reception building. Brilliant! Peggy offers to bring the donkeys into the barn during the service. Visions of Mary and Joseph on an actual donkey rise up before me. Goats, donkeys everywhere, on two occasions for Christmas.

All that is left is to bring this idea to the Sunday school coordinators and my worship committee. It may take some finesse, but who could resist a service in a barn with animals?

The only problem could be the weather. What if it snows? That could make the driving treacherous. On the other hand, it could just add that perfect touch, snow-covered fields. I wonder if Windreach Farms has horse-drawn sleighs?

But worrying is for later. Right now I have to get to the phones. I have meetings to arrange!

On the Third Day before Christmas,

Mother Nature gave to me

three feet of snow that blanketed

the enormous pine tree.

Wendy and the girls are in the middle of one of our family's great Christmas traditions. This tradition must be carefully timed to happen not too close and not too far away from Christmas Day. The accoutrements of this event are popcorn, tea, and my mom's Christmas cookies. Also essential: all the ringers on our various phones must be turned off. The lights in the family room are darkened, the television is turned on, a tape is slipped in, and voilà! We are watching Bing Crosby in *White Christmas*.

It is worth my life not to make a clever or amusing remark at any time during this movie. One witty phrase and I will be driven from the family room like a wolf being expelled from the pack. The three women in my life love this movie. I expect any year now that Sarah and Elizabeth are going to spontaneously burst into singing: "Sisters, sisters, there were never such devoted sisters. . . ."

But what is the crowning glory of this film? What is the event that brings the whole movie to a happy conclusion? Is it the sundered relationships reunited? No, it is the falling snow on Christmas Eve. Yes, a white Christmas, a snow-covered Christmas, that is what captures everyone's imagination. That is what is supposed to happen. For Christmas just isn't

Christmas without snow-covered rooftops, lights glittering off snowbanks, and trees encrusted with the white stuff.

Almost everyone wants snow. Retailers can track their Christmas sales from when the first flakes drop from the sky. The whole Canadian economy goes into a tailspin without a good blizzard. Travel agencies are empty unless snow drives customers in to arrange flights to warmer climes. Tow trucks and auto shops sit idly by if mild weather moves in. Ski resorts are empty, manufacturers of winter gear go into a slump, and ice fishers are forced to throw lines into their home freezers.

A winter without cold and snow is a catastrophe . . . for everybody but me. Yes, I alone do the dance for joy if there is no snow until after Christmas. Why am I so anti-frozen precipitation? The best way to answer that is to show what happened to church attendance during that last great blizzard we had.

On that Sunday, I woke up and looked out the front window. To my horror, three feet of snow surrounded both of my cars. The only sound besides the whistling of the wind was the howl of this minister, who had to go to work through this.

I ate breakfast and just after 7:30 a.m. was out shovelling. This, I was convinced, was sheer madness. No one would get through the blizzard to church. I was reminded of the question "If a tree falls in a forest and nobody hears, does it make a sound?" I wondered if the same question could be asked of a minister preaching a sermon to an empty church.

By just after 8:00 a.m., I had dug out the driveway enough that the car could make it to the road. Unfortunately, there wasn't a snowplough in sight, and for a moment I wondered if I would have to shovel a path to the main street. But, no, I was confident my car would make it. I loaded up shovel, salt, and extra mitts and clothes. I was ready for anything.

I am Canadian.

I started the car and backed it out into the street. The car stopped. The car did not like all this snow. The car wanted to go back to its cozy little resting place.

The tires spun enthusiastically, but that's all that moved. I was stuck three feet away from my own driveway and wasn't going anywhere.

But I am Canadian. What was being stuck in the snow to me? I rocked the car back and forth and slowly ground my way back onto my property.

What was I going to do about church? My cross-country skis and snowshoes were at the cottage. I was stranded. I thought of my great-grandfather, who was a Methodist minister in northern Alberta. He rode a horse in the dead of winter, wrapped up in a buffalo robe, to get to his church. Alas, I had neither buffalo robe nor horse. Curse those short-sighted zoning regulations. Didn't they realize this is Canada, where a horse may be needed at a moment's notice?

I phoned around. Everyone else was snowed in. I conferred with my chairpeople of worship and the official board. We came to a momentous decision: we cancelled church. The prospect of returning to bed and sleeping the rest of the morning was almost too painful to bear, but I was stoic.

I am Canadian.

I was just preparing to return to the boudoir to bury my sorrow in slumber when the phone rang. It was Larry, chairperson of the board. He suggested someone should go to the church and put up a sign. He offered to do so, for he had a four-wheel-drive pickup truck.

My conscience stirred. What if someone shows up? (Insert laughter here.) I called our retired organist, who was scheduled to fill in for our regular organist that Sunday. His wife told me he had already left. I took a moment's respectful silence, convinced he would never be seen again until spring thaw. Then I called Larry back.

"Bring your truck," I said. "In the spirit of my great-grandfather, we shall venture forth together. After all, we are Canadians."

I bid a regretful farewell to my pyjamas and threw on some pants, a sweater, and my boots.

Larry's truck arrived in a shower of snow. We charged through the blizzard and got to the entrance to the main road, where he pointed out that the snow-plough had ploughed the street in. I never would have made it to the church. We got there at 9:30, fifteen minutes after the first service was set to begin. We were not alone. Ron, the organist, had made it, and so had sixteen others. I was amazed. Not only were they there, but they also wanted a church service. Two of the men were even wearing suits! And these folks had made it without horses or four-wheel drives.

Only Canadians would make it to church in the worst blizzard in seven years. I ripped up the sign cancelling church and directed them all into the first three pews (why do people always sit at the back?).

The service was great. The smallest crowd I've ever preached to but great.

Would more come for the second service, I wondered? They did — another fifteen people arrived. We packed them into the front rows, and away we went again.

After church I was driven home in another parishioner's four-wheel drive. As we approached my house, I saw a sight guaranteed to warm the coldest Canuck heart. Wendy and the girls were out shovelling. I felt terrible disturbing them. Why break their rhythm and interrupt Wendy's cardiovascular work-out? That's not what a caring, sensitive husband would do.

"Let's go to lunch," I called out to my driver.

Too late, I was spotted.

Later, when we had finished the shovelling, our neighbours Mark and Julie invited us over for a late lunch, followed by a couple of games of euchre. We were cold and tired but happy. After all, we're Canadians. Snow is our natural habitat!

Don't misunderstand me — I love snow . . . after Christmas. For snow is not just precipitation; it is also a way of life. Tobogganing, snowmen, snow angels, snow forts, and snowball fights: these are the stuff of our childhood years, and it is amazing what can trigger memories of them.

I had lunch with my dad the other day, and on the way home I drove by my childhood home. I stopped the car and, under the gaze of mildly suspicious neighbours, just stared at it. New paint, beige instead of white. The old garage out back from which my sister would launch herself into space and where I would spend hours shooting tennis balls into a hockey net — all gone, torn down.

I drove over to my old school up the street. A new addition filled the courtyard where we used to play road hockey. Down the street past my junior high sat my high school, looking just as I remembered it. The ice rink had been flooded. A few people were playing a desultory pick-up hockey game. The low-rise apartments that I saw every day for twelve years had a slightly dilapidated look, and a rezoning sign out front announced their impending replacement with condos. Even the ravine behind the private girls' school where we had our illicit tree fort had been cleared up.

But though I registered all that, I saw something quite different.

My eleven-year-old self, on a winter's morning, all decked out in coat, hat, boots, and mitts. I wave goodbye to my parents and head out for the day with my battered aluminum toboggan. The snowbanks are high; the air is cold. I make my first stop at the north hill by my junior high. There, along with other kids with toboggans and wooden sleds with metal runners, I hurtle down the hill. The closer to the building, the steeper the hill. We charge bravely down and run back up. Then it is over to the south hill — the suicide run. This hill is steep and icy, trees on one side, railing on the other. At the bottom, dug out of the snow, is a jump that is rock solid. We fly into the air, land with a bone-jarring thump, and brag to each other about how we didn't feel a thing.

From there we go through the ravine, dragging our toboggans and pretending we are on an expedition to the Arctic, carrying vital relief supplies to the trapped residents of the town ahead of us. Our imaginary dogsleds acquire the whiff of authenticity when we draft the neighbourhood dogs into duty and try to get them to pull a toboggan. But they have grown soft. Their hearts aren't really in it. So we free them and throw snowballs for them to chase.

Then it is up the hill, across the street, and into the next park. This hill is steep. In the summer, the grass is trimmed and manicured. Thus, in winter, the slope is fast, very fast.

We load ourselves all onto one toboggan and use every pound for momentum and every arm for thrust. We gather speed like a roller coaster heading into the loop. With snow flying into our faces, we hit bottom, tumbling into each other, a profusion of arms and legs as the sleds turn over. Our real aim is to stay upright as long as possible so that we can see how far we can travel from the end of the hill into the park. We mark the completion of our forward path and do it again and again, entering into unofficial competitions with anyone else on the hill.

On we travel, across Yonge Street and into another park, pulling sleds, sliding down hills, tossing snowballs at each other until the light in the sky shifts into early twilight. Then back we go, retracing our steps, but with few if any stops. Snow is in our boots, our mitts are soaked, and our hats and scarves are covered in ice. The cold that earlier in the morning added just the right flavour to the day is now seeping into our bones. We keep moving, saying nothing now, and friends peel off to their own houses.

Finally, I climb the last hill. The houses are illuminated with bright Christmas lights, reflecting off the white snow in the yards. After dropping the toboggan off in the garage, I push open the side door and call out, "Hi, Mom. I'm home." Home: warm and fragrant with the smells of dinner in the stove. Boots are shaken outside to get rid of the snow. My socks are encrusted with miniature snowballs that start to melt in the hall. Off with them too. Coat, hat, and mitts are draped near the radiator, the smell of damp wool rising with the steam into the kitchen. On with dry pants and dry shirt and back downstairs for hot tea loaded with milk and sugar and some cookies to warm me up and hold me till dinner. A thump at the door heralds the arrival of the afternoon paper, and my sister and I begin our weekly negotiations over who gets the Saturday comics first. Dad, in the corner of the couch, surrounded by students' essays and exams, is marking intently. The living room fire roars. My sister and I spread the comics out in front of it and share the humour.

God is in his heaven, and all is right with the world.

I shook my head, and the vision passed. I started up the car and headed home, hoping to be there when the girls got back from school. A minute or two after I walked in the door, the girls entered: "Dad, we're home. Are we going tobogganing?" Whereupon begins the making of new memories.

With the arrival of winter, kids and sleds sprout at Pringle Park hill like crocuses in spring. Our toboggan trailing behind us, we join the throng on a Sunday afternoon.

Our plastic three-person toboggan has a few features that are a real improvement over my old aluminum rocket. First, it has short sides that keep you inside as you fly down the hill sideways. Second, it's fast — really fast. Which is great except that there is no cushion to comfort your lower extremities when you fly over the jump that some kid always builds at the bottom of the hill. The method of downhill transport that catches my fancy is the inflatable tube. Now that's the way to travel, floating downhill on a cushion of air, dismissive of bumps.

The old-fashioned sled is a thing of the past, replaced by GT racers that not only look cool but also have steering mechanisms that actually work. Tobogganing today is a high-tech affair, complete with camcorders recording every moment and dads on cellphones ordering pizzas for pickup on the way home. As we make our way to the top of the hill, we soon discover that the slope is not the only hazard to contend with. The hill resembles an expressway during rush hour. Kids and parents are jumping for their lives as racers and sleds make their descent.

Sarah, Elizabeth, and I jam ourselves together on our plastic chariot with me in the front nominally in charge of steering. I selected the steepest part of the hill, and with my knees up near my ears, Sarah in the rear, and Elizabeth crushed between the two of us, we cast off. Gravity is a wonderful thing: it keeps you from falling off the Earth. But the rules of gravity are suspended in a fast-moving toboggan. As our juggernaut gains speed, I notice that down below is a small, unsuspecting family. A hitherto happy family, revelling in the pleasure of a winter's afternoon. A family blissfully unaware of their approaching doom. In the front of my racing steed are ropes, placed there, theoretically, for steering. I grab them with the same desperate energy with which one grabs the bridle of a runaway horse. My attempts to shift us to the left make absolutely no difference. On we thunder. I quickly lean my body full over to the right. All that accomplishes is to aim the toboggan more to the centre, guaranteeing that if we hit the family there will be no survivors.

At this precise moment, the family look up at us with widening eyes. I prepare to abandon ship, sacrificing myself for others, hoping only for a small, decorous plaque with my name on it in remembrance of my heroic actions. There is only one problem with this plan. I'm stuck. I can't move. Centrifugal force, combined with the pressure of two teenagers, has caught me in a vice. All that is left is prayer. Then Sarah simply sticks her heel in the snow, and we careen safely past them.

After this weekend, I plan to contact the Canadian Olympic Association. I can guarantee it a bobsled team that will win gold at the next Winter Games.

One place where snow is an absolute requirement is the cottage in December. Nothing can match the beauty and wonder of snow-covered trees and lake in the Canadian north. And a cottage Christmas is an experience not to be missed. But a few such Christmases may be all we need, after the memorable one several years ago. We arrived first late Friday afternoon, parked the car by a four-foot snowbank, and trudged up the hill to the cottage. We arrived at the back door only to discover, to our shock and dismay, that we couldn't get in. Those wonderful people who shovel the snow off the roof so it doesn't collapse had shovelled it right onto the small deck at the side of the cottage and left it there to melt and freeze into an impenetrable wall that only a bulldozer could have gone through. This was our only port of entry because the screen door at the front had been locked from inside.

There are many things one might wish for when beginning a cottage Christmas. Please be assured that shelter and warmth are numbers one and two on the list.

The sun was setting, it was getting colder, my daughters and spouse were gathered around the front door demanding immediate entrance. I looked over my family — like small members of Scott's ill-fated expedition to the South Pole. I was sure Scott's trip had seemed like a good idea at the time, as well.

I walked back down through the snow to the car, grabbed the shovel, then attempted to hack, chop, and erode the ice wall. After twenty minutes of non-stop labour, the cold had disappeared for me, but I had excavated a passage that only a small child could get through. I threw the shovel to the ground in frustration and howled like a wolf. Even stripped to my long johns, there was no way I would get in. Wendy reproved me for my language in front of the girls. I testily explained that no adult could ever get through that passage. We would have to go to the nearest Holiday Inn until the next morning. Then, with the aid of a blowtorch, a backhoe, and some dynamite, we just might make it into the cottage for New Year's.

Wendy does not have a sarcastic bone in her body, but one appeared as if by magic. She pointed at the two small children shivering at her feet. "Only a small child could get through, eh? Do you think, just perhaps, that one of them might do?"

Silently, I passed Sarah the front door key and she wiggled through, opened the side door, disappeared, unlocked the screen door, and voila — we were in. I started a fire, turned on the heaters, ran the stove up to 500 degrees Fahrenheit, and went back with an axe to reduce the wall before unloading the rest of the car.

The next task was ensuring that we had fresh water. This would entail running to the lake with buckets and carrying water into the cottage. But before that, a hole in the ice had to be chopped. This was not a job that could wait until morning.

So down to the lake I trudged, buckets, sieve, axe, and flashlight in hand. No moon, just the stars and the freezing wind to keep me company. Have you ever tried to chop a hole in the ice with an axe near the end of a Canadian December? Intelligent people use gas-driven augers and wait until daylight. But for me there was only an axe. The first challenge, besides making sure all my limbs stayed attached, was making sure I consistently thrust the axe down in the same place instead of randomly whacking various parts of the lake. Doing this while holding a flashlight is not an insignificant accomplishment. I swung the axe a few times, cleared the ice away, and kept swinging.

On and on it went, and down and down went the hole. The ice gets darker and darker the deeper you go, a sure sign the end is near. People in deserts see the mirage of an oasis, with palm trees and glittering blue water; I started to imagine that every swing of the axe meant the water would soon be gushing through. I swung the axe, cleared away the ice, and peered intently with my flashlight into the growing hole. Did I see a trickle? Were all my labours at an end? With mounting frustration, I chopped and chopped. The anticipated exhilaration, the thrill that comes when you finally hear the gurgle of water and watch it stream through that hole in the ice, kept me going.

Exhausted, chest heaving, I rested for a moment. Just then my brother-in-law, Alan, came down to the lake, having just arrived for the family holiday. Terrific guy, Alan. We get along great. I bid him a feeble hello. Whereupon Alan took three swings with the axe, and the water poured through. He then smiled that smile of victory that comes with seeing a job well done, passed me the axe, and instructed his sons Jonathan and Jordie to cart the water up to the cottage. I stared with disbelief at the hole, then at Alan. I considered another use for the axe but was too tired to do anything other than skim out the ice and mark our hole with branches so nobody would drive a snowmobile over it.

The challenges were not over. Oh, no. The next one was entertainment. The temperature inside was barely higher than that outside. To keep the children amused while the cottage heated up, which would take until breakfast, I slipped a movie into the cottage VCR. It didn't work. All we got was static and a pathetic whirring noise. I immediately identified the problem: damp combined with cold is death to VCRs.

But I had an absolutely brilliant idea. "Heat," I said to myself. "If we could direct heat into the VCR, why, it would be dry and toasty, and the kids would be watching movies in no time." Thus emboldened, I propped ajar the VCR's opening and positioned the ceramic heater to blast its inferno right into the machine itself.

Feeling that even Albert Einstein would doff his hat to me this time, I headed outside with my flashlight to search for our canoe, which must have drifted onto someone else's property. I found it on the shore three lots down the lake, and about twenty minutes later I had triumphantly returned it to our cottage.

Upon entering the cottage, I noticed two things. First, the fragrant smell of wood smoke was mixed with another odour that I could not as yet identify, but it was not pleasant. Second, the television set had transformed into a new design, something like a combination of an iMac and a Volkswagen Beetle. It was retro curvy where before it had been straight and utilitarian. Equally strange to me were the new curves that had been adopted by the VCR. Then the proverbial penny dropped, and I realized that the heater was melting all of our audiovisual aids. Screaming curses that were not suitable for family hearing, I leapt to the TV and unplugged the heater. In a vain attempt to reposition the blame, I immediately castigated assorted relatives for not watching closely while I was gone. Not only did they refuse to accept responsibility for their thoughtless inaction, but my sister-in-law Cathy and my niece Megan couldn't stop laughing.

I don't know what the recommended internal temperature is for a VCR, but I do know ours was hot enough to cook a steak to medium rare. If I had put a tape in at that moment, the whole thing would have turned into Silly Putty. I decided that stuffing it with snow would be counterproductive and waited for it to cool down.

A few hours later we pried the VCR open and put in a tape. More static, combined now with the grinding sound of a VCR ingesting ribbons of video.

The good news was that the TV still worked. And three days of playing board games really does bring an extended family closer together. We also played cards, and I battled my girls, nephews, and niece in a new game called Spit. This is a card game that requires speed, accuracy, and great skill. As a result, I was massacred. We shovelled off a patch of thick ice near the shore, and between indoor games and eating we skated and skied in the bush.

When I think of Christmases we spent at the cottage when I was a boy, I remember Mom decorating the tree that Dad and I had chopped down in the woods; cross-country skis resting in snowbanks; the sounds of snowmobiles crossing the lake. And, of course, an event I would never live down.

I was sixteen years old, and we were up at the cottage for the week. We cross-country skied every day. We did not have a snowmobile, but my buddies did, and one morning three snowmobiles arrived at the top of the driveway to whisk me away for a day of adolescent adventure. I put on my snowmobile suit and boots, said a quick goodbye, and headed up the hill at full speed before my parents remembered that they needed me to chop wood and haul water up from the lake.

I had just gotten on the back of a snowmobile when the back door of our cottage opened. My mother appeared on the porch and started waving something at me. "Christopher . . . Christopher," she called in a maternal voice that overpowered the sounds of three revving snowmobiles. "You forgot your hat. Come and get it before you leave."

Oh, the humiliation! To have to walk down the hill in front of a pack of teenage boys. To pick up the hat and walk back up the hill with Mom waving happily away, innocent of the fact that I was now marked for life.

All day, all winter, and all the next summer, my friends inquired solicitously if I had my hat. To say that I never heard the end of it would be an understatement. The incident occurred twenty-nine years ago this winter. But my friends who have cottages on that lake still tell the story.

My elder daughter is now fourteen. While I have no doubt that I can and will embarrass her on other subjects, let me tell you her head is her own, come rain or snow.

I have only two days left to finalize preparations for the Christmas Eve services. And tonight is choir rehearsal time. I look out the window. Oh, no, it's snowing!

On the Second Day before Christmas,

the choir sounded to me

like two calling birds nesting

in the enormous pine tree.

Music is a powerful medium, one that affects us on many levels, emotionally, spiritually, even physically. Margaret, my church organist, tells me that, when we sing together in church or any public place, we start breathing together and that a bone in our ankles actually starts to resonate in a biological harmony. This confirms that singing is good for you: it lifts the heart and stirs the soul while reducing stress.

Who among us has been unmoved, late on Christmas Eve, when the lights dim in a church, and the candles are lit, and the congregation sings the world's most beloved carol, "Silent Night"? The only carol with its own web pages. A carol translated into 230 languages. A carol first performed by its author and his organist in a small Austrian mountain church in 1818. A simple but beautiful tune combined with inspired lyrics.

As with all things, even our beloved Christmas music has had its detractors.

The early church dismissed these songs as pagan and quite unsuitable for singing in church to mark the birth of Jesus. But the people loved them, so they persevered. Eventually, the songs entered into the seasonal life of worshipping communities. Stemming from the French word *carole* and the Latin *choraula* and the Greek *choros*, carol means a circling dance often accompanied by singing and associated with dramatic performances, religious festivities, and fertility rites.[2]

Fertility rites! Perfect, great, just what I need my youthful cast to hear! Who knows what they would want to present onstage if that nugget of knowledge made it into their Hotmail accounts! The mind boggles.

Carols have served a variety of purposes over the years, including political intrigue and a signal to launch a revolution. Take my favourite, "O Come, All Ye Faithful," a.k.a. "Adeste Fideles," which was written around the time of the 1745 Scottish rebellion of Bonny Prince Charlie. Since the author was a keen Jacobite sympathizer, it might have been used in its original Latin to rally people to the cause. The carol is filled with possible double entendres and even a pun that refers to Charles Stuart. On the surface, "Adeste Fideles" functioned as a Christmas carol, but underneath it sent a signal to the faithful of England, alerting them to the arrival of the Stuart prince, who was attempting to reclaim the English throne.

Illicit political undertones are also present in, of all carols, "The Twelve Days of Christmas." In its

[2]Ian Bradley, *The Penguin Book of Carols* (London: Penguin Music, 1999), ix.

original form, it may well have been used as an allegorical means of religious education for a persecuted church: ten lords a-leaping for the Ten Commandments; three French hens for the gifts of gold, frankincense, and myrrh left by the Magi; and two turtledoves for the two testaments of the Bible.

So when you open that hymnal in church, or your local newspaper's carol sheet, you never know exactly what you might be getting into!

Besides these Christmas favourites, another musical piece dominates the December landscape. Like Christmas lights and Santas in the mall, it can be found in every community, large or small, urban or rural. All of North America rings with its choruses and solos. I refer, of course, to the most famous oratorio on the planet: Handel's *Messiah*.

The *Messiah* is a combination of solo pieces and choruses sung by a choir. Handel wrote the music in just a few short weeks, after receiving the libretto from Charles Jennens, who had compiled it from the biblical story of Jesus. Handel realized he had something special, and it was first performed as a benefit concert in Dublin on Tuesday, April 13, 1742. (While originally meant for Lent, over the years the oratorio has become a Christmastime classic.) It was an immediate success. The oratorio as a musical form was gaining popularity as the general public tired of operas.

(Imagine that — and they had yet to hear Richard Wagner!)

Handel's popular new work was not without critics or controversy. Some were scandalized that scripture was put to music in this way (imagine their reactions to Andrew Lloyd Webber). Others objected to a sacred work being performed in theatres. Actors were considered, in some quarters, to be highly immoral and their places of work inappropriate for a piece of this significance to be presented. (All of which is highly ironic when you consider what people said about the person upon whose life this is based. He, too, was chastised for spending his time with "unsuitable" members of society.)

I am familiar with this piece not only as the husband of a *Messiah* soloist but also as a singer myself and as the marketing director of a choir that Wendy started a few years ago. She had decided that we needed a community choir for people who couldn't sight-read music but loved to sing. She began a nonaudition choir out of Durham College, our local community college. We started small. About thirty singers were part of that original cadre. The choir had the typical makeup of amateur and church choirs: sopranos and altos in plenitude, with a few hardy and courageous males singing bass and tenor.

When your spouse begins a new project like this, and you sing in your church choir, it behooves you in

the interests of tranquil domestic relations to participate enthusiastically. Thus, I joined the ranks of the
tenors (no, we were not rank). In the beginning, we
performed pieces that were not overly taxing but
were a lot of fun to sing, such as folk songs and
pieces in two-part harmony. We held concerts and
sang with other groups. And so it would have continued in blissful delight but for our friend Jurgen.
He had an idea, a bright idea, an idea that was both
inspired and generous. An idea for which I am only
now beginning to forgive him.

It was a warm, peaceful, late-spring night. We
were in the garden just finishing dinner. My roses
were blooming, my wisteria was in full purple splen-
dour, and the birds were trilling with enthusiasm.
With Jurgen's words, the birds migrated south, and
my roses turned into thistles. "Wendy," he said. "Why
don't we combine our choirs, and we'll come out
here and do the *Messiah* with you next Christmas?"

Now Jurgen conducts a classical choir in
Toronto. It contains professional singers and requires
the type of audition that would have sent our cho-
risters back to their showers for the rest of their
singing careers. I was filled with a nameless dread. I
saw our choir fleeing after seeing the first page of
the music. To go from singing simple folk songs to
singing the *Messiah* is like going from jumping into
a pile of leaves in your front yard to skydiving. Then

there was the cost of the orchestra, the venue, the soloists, publicity. Was there an audience out here? Could we sell tickets? Who would be in charge of that? How could we manage to get everything done between September, when the choir would re-form after the summer dispersal of its members, and December? Maybe we could be ready the year after; give us an extra year to learn the music. Yes, that's the idea: time, angle for time.

Just as I was fashioning an answer that would be encouraging without committing us to anything, my spouse responded, "Wonderful, Jurgen. We'll do it."

I wish to emphasize at this point that Wendy used the word *we'll*. "We'll," as in the plural of "I'll." A word that denotes not just one but at least two. A word that implies that a partner of twenty years will be intimately involved in the execution of this wonderful idea. And so it proved.

September rolled around, and at the choir's first rehearsal everyone was very excited. Enthusiasm boiled over as a recording of the *Messiah* by the Taverner Choir played in the background. This mood of joyous anticipation lasted until the following week, when we actually opened the music.

Have you ever seen a score to Handel's *Messiah*? The first thing that you notice are the notes. There are a lot of them, and they move all over the place. There are no unison parts. Everything is in complex four-part harmony. Imagine singing in a triathlon, and you will get the general idea. Handel loves speed; then he likes to slow down. He likes you to go to the highest point in your vocal range and then just for fun drop down to the lowest, while at the same time singing sixteenth notes as fast as your mouth can move. And as you are singing these impossible parts, hanging on for dear life, the other three parts are facing equally prodigious challenges.

Imagine the different parts as traffic on a freeway. Everything is flowing beautifully — until one vehicle blows a tire. Confusion and despair ensue as the freeway grinds to a halt while drivers ogle this one person change a tire. Now imagine all the vehicles blowing their tires one after the other.

Yes, that describes the first rehearsal. All right, to be accurate, it describes the first two months of rehearsals. The first chorus is called "And the Glory of the Lord." Glory was noticeably absent for quite some time. After only two pages, at about bar thirty-seven, it suddenly struck the choir what they were in for. Fear drove us, doubt moved in, and we all wondered if we could be ready in time.

Usually, at this point in the story, you'd expect to be given an explanation of how, through pluck and determination, the gang came through in the end.

Assume nothing.

As the fall progressed, I was drafted into the

glorious position of marketing director. This vaunted title implies power lunches with fellow artistes and meetings with the leading lights of our community to arrange huge endowments. In reality, my job was to push ticket sales. My sales force consisted of the choir singers themselves. Singers who were wondering if we could actually perform this piece in public. Singers who were unsure whether we were asking people to participate in an evening of sublime music that would transport their souls or an evening that would so negatively affect their Christmas spirit that they would join the ranks of Ebenezer Scrooge and the Grinch.

Preliminary sales figures soon laid to rest my fear of not having enough room in our venue. In its place was the reality of thousands of dollars worth of invoices and a near-empty house on the night of the performance. So I went into full gear, getting publicity wherever I could and cajoling my recalcitrant sales force like a sales manager whose team has not met their monthly targets for quite some time. I had three main pitches that evolved over those three months. Before making any of them, I would set the stage by writing on a blackboard the date and costs of the concert, beside that the number of tickets we needed to sell to meet those costs, and beside that our current sales figures. Our prospects reminded me of another of my favourite carols: "In the Bleak

Midwinter." "Bleak" was apt indeed. So it was time for my pitches.

Pitch one was my version of "Win one for the Gipper." It was a cheerleading pitch. "You can do it; I have faith in you; this is a great project; we're all working so hard; let's make sure that we have an audience to support this terrific music."

When cheerleading failed to generate the needed results, I moved on to the sorrowful pitch, which featured a sad shaking of the head combined with a mournful, disappointed expression. This suggested that I was struggling to understand why anyone involved in a concert such as this would not be selling tickets to everyone he or she knew, including distant cousins and the meter reader.

But my pièce de résistance, my show-stopper, was my last-ditch pitch. Solemn, serious, resigned, I simply announced that, if we did not have the required amount of revenue in the bank before the concert, I was going to cancel the whole thing to prevent us from winding up in enormous debt. Since I wasn't kidding, this pitch had the ideal combination of honesty and fear.

As the weeks went by, I sometimes resorted to all three pitches at once. It was a grim and thankless job. Choir members started to shun me, crossing the street if they saw me in town. But that didn't bother me in the least. I'd simply chase them into the grocery store and tackle them in the produce section to inquire about their ticket sales. They would brandish broccoli or a large cucumber to keep me at bay, but I was dogged in my pursuit.

Meanwhile, the rehearsals were, to say the least, a challenge. Each week Wendy would have the accompanist plunk out the parts, and we would try to put them together. Sometimes we managed to string together four or even five bars before we collapsed in exhaustion.

Wendy sang every part to every chorus into a tape recorder, made duplicate tapes, and handed them out to every singer who requested them. Morning, noon, and night we had the *Messiah* running through our heads. Weekend practices were mandated, and sectionals were held. But no matter how hard we worked, how late we stayed, one truth kept hitting us in the face: we were awful. Not just bad. Not just mediocre. No, we were truly, unrepentantly, ghastly. Ticket sales stalled because my choir members were embarrassed at the thought of people they knew hearing us sing.

Wendy and I started plotting a course for Plan B. Perhaps Jurgen's choir could carry the concert, and we would join them for a couple of choruses: "Hallelujah!," "Glory to God," simple stuff. There was always next year.

I read about an exchange Handel had with a choir

when he was rehearsing his first performance of the oratorio. One of the singers had problems with "And with his stripes." Handel swore at him in not one but four languages and exclaimed, "You scoundrel. Why didn't you tell me you couldn't sing a note?" I began to imagine the ghost of Handel rising from the grave, standing in front of our choir, and swearing at us in thirty different languages, threatening to strike us down with thunderbolts if we ever dared to sing in front of an audience.

Then, just when I was sure nothing could get worse, it did. Less than two weeks before the concert, Wendy developed laryngitis. Not only could our conductor not communicate with us, but she was also the mezzo-soprano soloist for the concert. This was not just a slight rasp in the throat. No, this was a full-blown case of the vanishing voice. She sucked throat lozenges, gargled with salt water, drank lemon juice and water by the gallon. Nothing, not even a whisper.

We gathered to rehearse anyway. With Wendy using sign language, we ran through the whole thing. We rose to our feet and sang chorus after chorus, nonstop, no corrections. At the end, Wendy was speechless. Sadly, we wished we were all speechless. At the break, people were rushing up to her hoping to catch her virus.

For Wendy, her voice loss was a catastrophe. In desperation, she travelled into Toronto to consult with the best specialist in the field. His office walls were covered with photographs of famous performers, all of whom attested to his skills and abilities. He examined her throat and put a scope down to her vocal chords to look at video pictures of them. Years of medical training allowed him to make an instant diagnosis: "You have laryngitis. Just rest your voice; that's all that can be done."

Monday, six days to go. We had all driven into Toronto and were with Jurgen's choir for the dress rehearsal. Two days before, Jurgen had come to lead our choir. He was reassuring. We were embarrassed. He was confident. We were terrified. He was hopeful. We were sceptical. But now a slight sliver of hope began to dawn. We rose up and sang with Jurgen's choir, the two groups carefully mixed together.

It was then that our choir understood the full meaning of the term "miracle." Singing with an experienced group who knew this music backward was a whole new experience. They carried us through. We discovered notes we never knew existed. They filled our gaps. Instead of dragging them down to our level, we rose up to theirs. Okay, let's be brutally honest: we rose to an acceptable level. But the transformation was remarkable. We stood tall at the break. We were no longer a struggling amateur choir; we were professionals. We were singers even Handel could accept.

Ticket sales skyrocketed, and I started to sleep again. But with five days to go, Wendy still had no voice. With nothing to lose, she saw a nurse who practises therapeutic touch. During the session, Wendy actually felt warmth in her throat, and twenty-four hours later her voice started to return.

Saturday morning, one last rehearsal. Good news: there was absolutely no danger that we would peak too soon. But even without the other choir, we sounded less awful. We had moments that were quite passable, one or two of them on the verge of being good.

Sunday afternoon I arrived at the venue. The choir turned in more ticket revenues. We were facing the distinct possibility of being able to pay the professional musicians. We rehearsed with the soloists and the orchestra. It was amazing. There we were, people who just loved music, who maybe used to sing in a choir, or currently sang in a church choir, and suddenly we were onstage with professional musicians! The performance depended on us, on what we brought to it, our skill, our talent. It was at that moment that I realized what my Wendy had given to these people, the Christmas gift she had lovingly presented to her choir all those months ago. Here were people who in their wildest dreams couldn't see themselves onstage like this, yet here they were. Their faces shone, and their excitement was palpable.

Just before the concert started, I hurried to the

lobby. People were coming in. They were picking up and purchasing tickets. The parking lot was backed up. It was going to work!

At 7:00 p.m., we all trooped into the hall. Jurgen, resplendent in full white tie and tails, grinned at us and lifted his baton, and we were off (some of us really were). From "And the Glory of the Lord" to the sublime "Surely," in which the tenor part soars to glorious heights, through to "Hallelujah!" we sang our hearts out.

The hallelujah chorus is the best-known section of the *Messiah*. Everybody is familiar with its rousing sounds. At every performance, the audience stands for this part, a practice that goes back to the first time royalty was present at its performance. King George III of England was so moved by the absolute power of the singers that he stood to pay tribute during the singing of this portion of Handel's work. Because he was king, when he stood, everybody stood. Thus, a tradition was born.

That's one version. Jurgen has another. George stood up all right, but it was because the *Messiah*, in its original form, was of such great length that the king assumed this grand piece signalled the finale and was getting up to head to the door and go home. Personally, I'll go with the first version.

The time came for Wendy to sing. From a voice that was only a cackle a few short days before emerged her rich mezzo-soprano. Her rendition of "He Shall Feed His Flock" gave me goosebumps.

The *Messiah* concludes with the powerful "Worthy" and the final "Amen." It was absolutely glorious. Was it the best *Messiah* ever performed? Probably not. It had flaws and gaps, and we were not always in tune. But having sung this piece numerous times and more musically than at that performance, I know that something truly special happened that day. For all of us, whatever our faith, the power of the music, the lyrics, and the experience touched our lives as no other.

King of Kings! And Lord of Lords! And He Shall Reign Forever and Ever.

Hallelujah! Hallelujah!

On the *Last Day* before Christmas,

I paused and gave great thanks

for the manger

under the enormous pine tree.

It's early on the morning of December 24, just before the sun rises. I go downstairs, open the front door to a chill blast of wind, grab the paper, and shut the door as fast as I can. I plug in the Christmas tree, put on some festive music, sit in the big red wing chair, and look over at the brightly lit tree that seems to fill the house. The two books that we read aloud every Christmas Eve in between church services, *The Night before Christmas* and *Christmas!* by Peter Spier, are sitting on the footstool, ready and waiting.

Wendy's homemade stockings, bright red, with our names sewn on them, and each one large enough to hold an RV, are laid out, ready to be filled. Presents of curious shapes and sizes sit under the branches, impatient for the next day.

My sister, Alison, still groggy from jet lag, staggers upstairs and puts on the kettle. She knows that in less than twenty-four hours her two nieces are going to explode into her room calling out "Auntie Alison, Auntie Alison, get up, it's Christmas!" Trudy's sticky bun, one of the summer's last, sits out on the kitchen counter, thawing, to be devoured between opening stockings and presents.

The girls come downstairs and stare at the presents, trying to make out which are theirs and what they might contain. They head off to the kitchen, where the sound of cereal being poured mixes with excited voices. Wendy stays upstairs for as long as possible. We have a very long day ahead of us.

The phone rings, the first of many calls: Dad confirming his arrival time for the next day, Alan and Cathy seeing what time we will be over for our visit in the afternoon, an anxious cast member, double- and triple-checking when he needs to be at the church.

I feel, as I do each Christmas Eve, that particular combination of exhaustion, exhilaration, and anticipation. Christmas, my Christmas, starts right now. Over the next few hours, I go over the scripts and the services (two showings of our Christmas play, one candlelight service), review the music, answer more phone calls, double-check the menu and the ingredients for tomorrow's meal, review my sermon, and call my good friend Larry to confirm the goat and pizza delivery. I eat lunch, shower, get dressed, and by 2:30 p.m. am at the church.

The building is not large. It is a classic postwar church constructed in 1959 as a gym, with the idea that the main sanctuary would be added a few years later. That portion was never built. The land was used instead for a housing project for seniors. But an addition to the existing building was completed in 1992. The seating is a mixture of pews in the old building, mismatched chairs in the balcony, and yet another set of chairs in the side room on the left as you walk in. There are some unique, beautiful, stained glass windows in the west window.

I have spent the majority of my working life as a minister in this building. I know its shortcomings. Poor sight lines, a cramped front, suspect acoustics, bizarre heating patterns, and an electronic organ that was good for its time. But this space holds a unique place in my heart, and I will miss it, for this will be our last Christmas in this building. We are moving, all of us, to a new, badly needed, larger facility that will be erected a little way to the north. The plans are displayed in the lobby, and, after much hard work, we have the funds to begin the project, now that this facility is sold. I'm glad it will remain a house of worship for another denomination. We are not abandoning it; we are passing it on to a new community who will care for it.

The church is empty when I arrive. I walk in, turn on the lights, plug in the Christmas tree, and open the doors. I walk through every square inch of the sanctuary, like a hockey player skating around a rink to get the feel of the ice before the big game. I sit at the back, then in the balcony, and finally in the worst seat in the house, the back right corner of our overflow room.

I imagine tonight's production, playing it

through, scene by scene, in my head. I walk up to the chancel and deliver my sermon for the late service, using the small platform built for me at the front. I walk around as I preach — apparently, I look like a caged animal when I try to stay behind the pulpit. I listen to the cadence of my words, to how the phrases I have written sound when transferred from paper to voice. I change a couple of lines, rearrange the order of one or two sections, preach it again, and make a few more changes. Then it's ready.

I can see cars slowing down outside, checking the service times. The phone rings constantly with people calling to inquire when the proceedings begin. I sit for one last peaceful minute, soaking up the atmosphere, a final quiet pause before the storm. By 3:00, I can hear the chatter of teenagers as my cast arrives. They go downstairs, where our makeup artist, Shiona, has set up her table. The boys look mildly uncomfortable at first as they see themselves transformed but soon are taken with the feeling of being professionals. The energy in the room climbs as costumes are donned and lines reviewed, and conversations spring up about how many family members are coming. My techie, Kyle, and I head upstairs to turn on the spotlights and do a sound check.

The cast assemble at the front of the church. Their adrenaline levels are so high they are in danger of bouncing through the roof. Lisa leads them through the choreography, which settles them down. We do a quick walk-through of the play, with me shouting "Thank you, next scene," at thirty-second intervals. Costume changes are checked, props are put in their places, and by 4:00 everyone is downstairs. A small crowd has been gathering by the front door since 3:45, waiting for the doors to open so the people can get their seats. Christmas Eve is the only time of the year when church resembles a rock concert with fans scrambling for their places. And scramble they do. By 4:30 the place is packed. By 4:40 we open the choir stalls to the public. By 4:45 a sign goes on the front door announcing with great regret that the inn is filled; folks can wait downstairs or return for the 7:00 p.m. service.

At 4:45 I call the cast together in the basement. Flashes go off as pictures are taken. My kids can't believe how many people have come to see them. Before we head upstairs for showtime, we must thank some special people. Flowers for Margaret, our organist; Shiona, our makeup artist; Lisa, our choreographer; and Marissa, our youth coordinator. Then a presentation of the traditional stuffed sheep or goat to the cast members heading off to college or university.

Finally, a quiet reminder from me about the significance of what the cast is doing tonight, about what makes this different from any school play the kids have ever done. About how this evening makes

Christmas real for all those people. We link hands for a short prayer, and then it's places everyone!

Upstairs the church hums with anticipation. Babies cry, children speak in high-pitched voices, and parents try to maintain a modicum of control. Margaret fires up the organ, the swells of "O Come, All Ye Faithful" fill the sanctuary, and we're off.

As I get to the front of the sanctuary, I see the only spare space in the building is at my pulpit. I'm glad that someone didn't try to scalp that! I welcome people, remind them that it's Christmas, and tell them not to worry about keeping excited children quiet. We sing carols, read scripture. Then I move to the back, the lights dim, and the play begins.

The play is wonderful. Lines are missed, but the other characters keep going as if absolutely nothing is wrong. Entries and exits are made on time, and everybody is in sync during the dance sequence. As we near the end, I see Larry and Syd, dressed in their shepherd costumes, trailing goats. A loud "maaaa" is heard. Mary and Joseph are cued. In they go with shepherds, wise men, and the goats. The cardboard on the sanctuary floor is put to good use, and the children crane their necks to get the best view. The biblical Christmas story from Luke's gospel is read:

> And there were in the same country shepherds abid-
> ing in the field, keeping watch over their flock by

night. And, lo, the angel of the Lord came upon them, and the glory of the Lord shone round about them: and they were sore afraid. And the angel said unto them, Fear not: for, behold, I bring you good tidings of great joy, which shall be to all people. For unto you is born this day in the city of David a Saviour, which is Christ the Lord. And this shall be a sign unto you; Ye shall find the babe wrapped in swaddling clothes, lying in a manger. (King James Version)

We sing "Silent Night" and make our exit. I shake hundreds of hands, wish everyone a Merry Christmas. I am thrilled with the smiles and the comments on how this annual event helps to make Christmas real. We clean up the mess from the first service, go downstairs for pizza, pop, and Timbits, and go over what went well and what needs to be tweaked.

Before we know it, people start arriving for the 7:00 p.m. service.

The church is full again, but this time we have room for everybody. The 7:00 crowd is a little more subdued, the children quieter, but there is still a buzz in the room. The organ starts, and we're off again. This performance is almost word perfect. I stand by the doors and enjoy every minute, revelling in what we have done together. Before I know it, far too quickly, the service is over. Another play enters into our collective history.

Then the big cleanup begins. The cardboard is rolled up, windows are opened to release the barnyard emanations, props are taken down, the communion table is set up, the vacuum is put to good use, and the chairs at the side are straightened up. Crumpled orders of worship are picked up, and the flotsam and jetsam of the two services are tidied away.

With everything in place, I drive home. I have about an hour before I must go back to the church for the 10:30 p.m. service.

The girls are waiting for me. The stockings have been hung, and the big red chair beckons. We cuddle together, and I open the first book: "'Twas the night before Christmas, when all through the house not a creature was stirring, not even a mouse." I never tire of the wonderful old story.

We leave the eggnog for Santa and a carrot for Rudolph on the table by the stockings, and I tuck Lizzy into bed with the reminder that Christmas morning starts at 7:00 a.m. and not one second sooner. I hug Sarah, say good night, and wrap some presents. Well, "wrapping" might be a slight over-statement; I stuff them into gift bags, a wonderful new method of gift delivery invented either by a man or by a woman married to a man with wrapping skills similar to mine. I place the gifts under the tree, change into a clean shirt, and head back into the living room. Wendy and I say goodbye to my sister and drive back to the church.

If the early services are all noise and chaos, the 10:30 service is hushed and reverent. The sanctuary glows with candles, people speak in whispers, a sense of holiness fills the building. The lights are kept low as the people enter. The sense that we are celebrating the most sacred of moments is with us. We sing our first carol, greet each other, and pray, and then Wendy stands at the front and sings "O Holy Night."

> *Fall on your knees! Oh, hear the angel voices!*
> *O night divine, the night when Christ was born.*

The music comes from within her very soul, and its power moves people to tears. It's quite a challenge for this preacher to follow his spouse's music, for what can I say that will match the glory of this ancient story, heard in word and song?

But I do speak, of the mystery and the wonder that lie within us all. Of the vulnerability of this child, and of how God has caressed the Earth in a way that reaches into that most common and miraculous of human experiences: the birth of a child, the birth of hope itself. For what is Christmas but hope? Hope that our hurts will be healed, hope that our world will hear the angels' song of peace. Hope that on this night, of all nights, their song will truly be heard.

Then we break the bread and share the cup of communion, and the service is completed. Everyone holds a lit candle in a darkened church and sings "Silent Night." Quietly, reverently, people file out, their voices soft.

We wish each other a Merry Christmas, turn off the lights, lock the front door of the church, and head home.

The streets are quiet, with houses and buildings illuminated by strings of light. We can see rows of cars parked by the other churches we drive past, and, behold, the dreaded snow that has held off till now has just started to drift down from the sky.

It is close to midnight when Wendy and I get home. The house is silent. We put on our dressing gowns, do the final wrapping, and silently place the last gifts under the tree. Off go the lights, and we slip up to our room. I crawl under the blankets and experience the excitement that has been with me ever since I first had Christmas memories. How will the girls react to their gifts? How will Wendy react to the surprise that my daughters and I have been so carefully planning? What fiendish puzzle will my sister inflict on me this year? Will she be able to conquer the puzzle I have purchased for her?

I lie still, looking forward to the family gathering

for dinner, the laughter, the surprises, the silly paper hats and the awful jokes in the Christmas crackers, which nobody can ever open properly or get to pop on cue.

But just before sailing off to a much-deserved sleep, I am struck by how much I — we — have been given. Our family, like all families, has had its share of sorrow and worry. But joy has far outweighed it.

The Christmas that we celebrate is really two Christmases. When the early church chose the 25th of December to mark the birth of Jesus, it attempted to transform the Roman holiday of Saturnalia into a Christian celebration. The result was a tension between the sacred and the secular that exists to this day. But there is room for both, for the stable and the feast, the manger and the presents. I love it all.

May your family find peace, joy, and hope this Christmas season, in the twelve days before, and throughout the year to come.

Merry Christmas
from our family to yours.